W9-BNG-272

HIP-HOP
ARTISTS

CHILDISH GAMBINO

MULTIFACETED ARTIST

BY LAURA K. MURRAY

Essential Library

An Imprint of Abdo Publishing
abdobooks.com

ABDOBOOKS.COM

Published by Abdo Publishing, a division of ABDO, PO Box 398166, Minneapolis, Minnesota 55439. Copyright © 2020 by Abdo Consulting Group, Inc. International copyrights reserved in all countries. No part of this book may be reproduced in any form without written permission from the publisher. Essential Library™ is a trademark and logo of Abdo Publishing.

Printed in the United States of America, North Mankato, Minnesota.
102019
012020

THIS BOOK CONTAINS
RECYCLED MATERIALS

Cover Photo: Al Powers/Powers Imagery/Invision/AP Images
Interior Photos: NBC/Photofest, 4, 9, 22, 29, 58–59; Michael Kovac/WireImage/Getty Images, 12–13; Imeh Akpanudosen/Getty Images Entertainment/Getty Images, 16; Tom Watkins/Rex Features, 19; Shea Walsh/AXE/AP Images, 20; Featureflash Photo Agency/Shutterstock Images, 25; Jordan Strauss/Invision/AP/Rex Features, 30; Frazer Harrison/Getty Images Entertainment/Getty Images, 32–33; Gary Miller/WireImage/Getty Images, 34; Jack Plunkett/Time Warner Cable Music/AP Images, 40; FilmMagic/Getty Images, 43; Gregg DeGuire/FilmMagic/Getty Images, 44; Kevin Winter/Coachella/Getty Images Entertainment/Getty Images, 48; Lev Radin/Shutterstock Images, 51; Gabriel Grams/Getty Images Entertainment/Getty Images, 55; Charles Sykes/Invision/AP Images, 56–57; Vivien Killilea/MTV/Getty Images Entertainment/Getty Images, 63; Frank Micelotta/Picturegroup/Rex Features, 66; FX Networks/Photofest, 68; Chris Pizzello/Invision/AP Images, 72; Walt Disney Studios Motion Pictures/Photofest, 76; Stuart C. Wilson/Getty Images Entertainment/Getty Images, 78–79; Rich Fury/iHeartMedia/Getty Images Entertainment/Getty Images, 83; Michael Loccisano/MTV/Getty Images Entertainment/Getty Images, 85; Scott Garfitt/Rex Features, 87; Sky Cinema/Shutterstock Images, 88; Alberto E. Rodriguez/Disney/Getty Images Entertainment/Getty Images, 92–93; Walt Disney/Kobal/Rex Features, 94; Shutterstock Images, 96

Editor: Megan Ellis
Series Designer: Laura Graphenteen

LIBRARY OF CONGRESS CONTROL NUMBER: 2019942071
PUBLISHER'S CATALOGING-IN-PUBLICATION DATA

Names: Murray, Laura K., author.
Title: Childish Gambino: multifaceted artist / by Laura K. Murray
Other title: multifaceted artist
Description: Minneapolis, Minnesota : Abdo Publishing, 2020 | Series: Hip-hop artists | Includes online resources and index.
Identifiers: ISBN 9781532190193 (lib. bdg.) | ISBN 9781532176043 (ebook)
Subjects: LCSH: Childish Gambino, 1983- (Donald Glover)--Juvenile literature. | Actors--Juvenile literature. | Comedians--Juvenile literature. | Rap (Music)--Juvenile literature. | Songwriters--Juvenile literature. | DJs (Disc jockeys)--Juvenile literature.
Classification: DDC 782.421649--dc23

CONTENTS

Chapter ONE

"THIS IS AMERICA"

Around midnight on May 5, 2018, audience members filled Studio 8H inside New York City's famous 30 Rockefeller Plaza skyscraper. They were watching the week's episode of *Saturday Night Live* (*SNL*), which was being broadcast live to 2.8 million people watching on TV. Standing in front of the audience, actor Daniel Kaluuya announced, "Once again, Childish Gambino," before the camera shifted to the rapper on stage.[1] For his second musical performance of the night—a debut of his new song "This Is America"—Childish Gambino was shirtless and wearing light colored pants. Two gold necklaces hung around his neck. He stood straight-faced behind the microphone with his hands behind his back.

The music began. Childish Gambino sang a slow and melodic tune as smiling dancers in school uniforms moved energetically around the stage. Laser lights cut

When Childish Gambino performed "This Is America" on *Saturday Night Live*, he wore an outfit similar to the one he wore in the music video.

CHART-TOPPING DEBUTS

"This Is America" became the thirty-first song in history to debut at Number 1 on *Billboard*'s Hot 100 chart. Childish Gambino's song was the third Number 1 debut in a row, immediately following Drake's "Nice" and "God's Plan." Later in the year, Ariana Grande's "Thank U, Next" debuted at Number 1. The record four Number 1 debuts were actually a tie with 1995. That year, the Hot 100 chart saw four Number 1 debuts in a row: Michael Jackson's "You Are Not Alone," Mariah Carey's "Fantasy," Whitney Houston's "Exhale (Shoop Shoop)," and Mariah Carey and Boyz II Men's "One Sweet Day."

across the room and the beat changed to pulsing trap, a style combining hip hop and electronic. "This is America," Childish Gambino intoned, standing still. "Don't catch you slippin' up."[2] The dancers threw money in the air as blue and red lights flashed.

As Childish Gambino sang about gun violence, police, and racism in the United States, he slowly began moving to the beat. Soon he was dancing within beams of light, layering vocals over the lyrics, "Get your money, black man."[3] As the music and lights faded, a lone girl remained dancing onstage. The audience, quiet for most of the performance, burst into applause and cheers as the show went into commercial break.

Just before the *SNL* performance began, Childish Gambino had uploaded the official music video for "This Is America" to his YouTube channel. Directed by Childish

Gambino's frequent collaborator Hiro Murai, the video features the artist in an outfit similar to the one he wore on *SNL*. He and uniformed dancers move smoothly through a stark warehouse, passing scenes of horrific violence that contrast with their energetic dance moves. The video ends with its star running toward the camera. His eyes are wide with terror. In the background, indistinct figures run after him. As Childish Gambino wrapped up his *SNL* appearance, the music video was racking up views at an astonishing rate.

HIRO MURAI

Born in 1983 in Tokyo, Japan, Hiro Murai moved to California with his family at age nine. He graduated from the University of Southern California's School of Cinematic Arts before making a name for himself directing music videos for artists such as Earl Sweatshirt, A Tribe Called Quest, B.o.B., and the Shins. Murai's partnerships with Glover expanded from music videos to short films and eventually acclaimed television episodes. On working with Glover, Murai commented, "We've kind of chased that feeling of 'I don't know what it is yet, but this feels good.'"[4]

RENAISSANCE MAN

Childish Gambino is the musical alter ego of Donald Glover. Raised in Stone Mountain, Georgia, about 20 miles (32 km) east of Atlanta, Glover had been steadily gaining recognition for his creative talents and cross-genre successes in television, film, comedy, and music. He seemed to have an uncanny ability to excel at anything he tried.

It appeared that Glover could not get enough of creating, no matter what industry he was in. Although he seemed to move smoothly between rapping, acting, writing, and running his own television show, it wasn't always easy to find support for his many projects. He encountered skepticism from those who doubted his ideas and criticism from those who found his portrayals offensive and subject matter too controversial.

DOUBLE DUTY

Glover was both hosting and performing on *SNL* that night. Other stars who have joined *SNL* as both the guest host and musical performer have included Ray Charles, the Rolling Stones, Stevie Wonder, Dolly Parton, Britney Spears, Jennifer Lopez, Janet Jackson, Elton John, Lady Gaga, Miley Cyrus, Drake, and Ariana Grande, among others. At the time of Childish Gambino's 2018 appearance, Justin Timberlake held the record for most double-duty hosting gigs, appearing on the show in 2003, 2006, and 2013.[5]

THE WORLD REACTS

Despite his successful entertainment career, many people first took notice of Glover and his alter ego in May 2018 when he pulled double duty on *SNL*, acting as both host

Glover opened the episode of *SNL* with a comedic monologue. He also appeared in several sketches throughout the show.

and musical guest. Within 24 hours, the "This Is America" music video had gained nearly 13 million views on YouTube.[6] Written by Glover, Swedish composer Ludwig Göransson, and Jeffery Lamar Williams (also known as Young Thug), the song included vocals by Young Thug, 21 Savage, Quavo, Slim Jxmmi, and BlocBoy JB.

Childish Gambino's fame skyrocketed in the week following his *SNL* performance and his video release. "This Is America" debuted at Number 1 on the *Billboard* Hot 100 chart, ending Drake's 15-week reign at the top. It also took the Number 1 spot on the Hot R&B/Hip-Hop Songs and Hot Rap Songs charts. It was the first Childish Gambino song to make it into the top ten. "This Is America" also topped the streaming and sales charts for the week. According to *Billboard*, sales of Childish Gambino's previous albums rose 419 percent in the United States. His songs' collective video and audio streams received more than 102 million clicks.[7]

Critics, celebrities, and other listeners took to blogs and social media to comment on the "This Is America" video or offer their interpretation of its symbols and meanings. Many praised the song's commentary on controversial and

LUDWIG GÖRANSSON

Ludwig Göransson was born in 1984 in Sweden. He graduated from Stockholm's Royal College of Music and the University of Southern California's Scoring for Motion Picture and Television program. Göransson began partnering with Donald Glover in 2010 when both were working on the show *Community*, Göransson as the composer and Glover as an actor. The two have collaborated many times since, including on Childish Gambino's studio albums. As a composer, Göransson worked on films including 2018's *Black Panther*, for which he traveled to Africa to research traditional music. He won the Academy Award for Best Original Score for his work on the film.

uncomfortable realities, including the role of guns in America, police brutality, and the experiences of black people in the United States. "It turned the mirror on this country and said 'see your life,'" wrote online music critic Luvvie Ajayi. She continued: "It is a read, an indictment, and a challenge."[8] Musical artist and actress Janelle Monáe tweeted simply: "Donald. Glover." Her tweet eventually amassed more than 47,000 likes.[9] Others criticized the song for being politically charged and for its brutal depictions of violence.

> "America, I just checked my following list and/You go tell somebody/You . . .owe me."[11]
> — Young Thug, "This Is America"

It wasn't the first time that Glover's work had attracted forceful responses. For years, Glover had built his career on the idea of unpredictability and the practice of defying expectations and stereotypes, including those placed upon rappers and black men. Glover felt a responsibility to give a voice to the experiences of African Americans. "Part of the reason I do what I do is because I'm the only one who can do it," he told *Esquire* in 2018.[10] The world was ready to take notice.

LOOKING TO SAVE THE WORLD

Born on September 25, 1983, at Southern California's Edwards Air Force Base, Donald McKinley Glover was raised in Stone Mountain, Georgia, from age four. His father, Donald Glover Sr., was a postal worker. His mother, Beverly, was a daycare provider. In 1990, Donald's brother Stephen was born. The brothers became close friends.

The family took in dozens of foster children over the years and adopted two. Seeing the circumstances from which some of the children came had a profound effect on Donald as he grew up. Through those interactions, he was exposed to violence, drugs, and death.

Donald embraced the power of his imagination to cope with difficult situations and stand out in the busy household. He created stories, performed puppet shows, and experimented with music and rap. "I wanted to build my own world because then you get to make the world a

Donald's career took off when he was in his early 20s.

13

little safer," he remembered later.[1] When Donald was 11 years old, he wrote a letter to himself: "I'm gonna try and I'm gonna save the world."[2]

The Glovers were Jehovah's Witnesses. Following the rules of their religion, they did not celebrate birthdays or holidays. They also limited their children's exposure to pop culture and television. In secret, Donald taped episodes of the animated TV show *The Simpsons* on a voice recorder and listened to them in bed before falling asleep. He decided he wanted to write for the show when he grew up. He and Stephen dreamed up ideas for shows and movies that they might make someday.

STONE MOUNTAIN

Glover's hometown of Stone Mountain, Georgia, influenced his later projects and even served as the title to one of his mixtapes. The town was well known as the location of the largest Confederate monument in the country and was mentioned by name in Martin Luther King Jr.'s "I Have a Dream" speech. According to Glover, "If people saw how I grew up, they would be triggered. Confederate flags everywhere. . . . I saw that what was being offered on *Sesame Street* didn't exist."[3] When national debates grew over Confederate monuments in the late 2010s, some politicians and citizens called for the removal of the monument at Stone Mountain.

FINDING HIS PLACE

As he grew up, Donald found himself feeling like

an outcast. He didn't seem to fit any particular mold or stereotype. He was not only a self-professed "nerd" but also an African American Jehovah's Witness in a town with a large population of more mainstream Christians. He later recalled, "It was layer after layer of, 'You're a weirdo.' They just didn't have anywhere to put me."[4]

Donald found a refuge and outlet in music. He devoured a wide range of styles, from rap to rock to R&B to alternative. Rap particularly helped express his feelings of being a misfit. Initially, he tried to replicate the styles of popular rappers, such as Bone Thugs-n-Harmony and the Notorious B.I.G. When Donald tried freestyling, he was influenced by rap

MUSIC FAN

Glover has never shied away from experimenting with different types of music. Growing up, he listened to electronic, rock, and rap groups such as Kraftwerk, Korn, Limp Bizkit, No Doubt, and Slipknot, as well as soulful singers like Marvin Gaye, Lauryn Hill, and Stevie Wonder. In middle school, he was a fan of Kris Kross, a successful Atlanta-based rap duo starring teenagers Chris "Mac Daddy" Kelly and Chris "Daddy Mac" Smith. Glover went so far as to mimic the duo's clothing style by wearing yellow overalls to school. Glover also enjoyed eclectic artists such as Icelandic singer-songwriter Björk. He later commented, "Björk literally changed everything for me musically."[5]

Glover developed his own music style after listening to a wide variety of genres.

rooted in dark subject matter such as crime and violence. But the results didn't sound genuine to him.

A turning point came when Donald heard the 1995 song "I Wish" by Skee-Lo, whose lyrics came from the point of view of an outsider. According to Glover, that was the first time he understood the idea of "just rap about— or just do, in any art form—what you know, and that will make you you."[6] From then on, Donald felt the freedom of not having to pretend with rapping. Instead, he used rapping as a medium to discover who he was and what defined him as a person.

At his mother's insistence, Donald enrolled in DeKalb School of the Arts, a high school that focused on the performing arts. For his audition, he performed a monologue from the 1986 film *Ferris Bueller's Day Off* and sang a song by Boyz II Men. The school gave Donald the opportunity to try acting, playwriting, and music. He took the stage in various plays and musicals, earning a reputation for his humor and creativity. Aligning with his childhood dream, his classmates voted him "Most Likely to Write for *The Simpsons*."[7]

A GALAXY FAR, FAR AWAY

One pop-culture standby embraced by the Glover household was the Star Wars franchise. As a child, Glover owned action figures of Darth Vader and Lando Calrissian. The latter was particularly important to Glover, as Calrissian, played by Billy Dee Williams, was the only onscreen black character with a speaking role in the original trilogy. Later, black actors portrayed key characters in the prequel and sequel trilogies, including Samuel L. Jackson as Mace Windu, Lupita Nyong'o as Maz Kanata, and John Boyega as Finn. Glover himself would eventually portray Lando Calrissian in the 2018 film *Solo: A Star Wars Story*.

CHILDISH GAMBINO IS BORN

After graduating high school, Glover attended the Tisch School of the Arts at New York University (NYU) with the intention of becoming a playwright. College also served as a fertile environment for exploring music. Glover created his own songs and collaborated with other students, including classmate Chaz Kangas, for freestyle rap sessions in the dorms. He also DJed. He produced and remixed music as MC DJ or MC D. In 2002, he produced and released his first rap mixtape, *The Younger I Get*. Glover's classmates did not give it a positive reception. Many viewed the tracks as too personal and too far removed from the subjects of women, guns, and money that were popular in rap at the time.

Glover was still working to find a sound and

UPRIGHT CITIZENS BRIGADE

New York's Upright Citizens Brigade Theatre was founded in 1999 by comedians Matt Besser, Amy Poehler, Ian Roberts, and Matt Walsh. The four moved from Chicago to New York in 1996 and formed an improvisational and sketch comedy group that quickly grew into a comedy powerhouse. After creating a training program for new comedic talent, they developed a string of successful sketch television shows. The troupe's Los Angeles location opened in 2005, and additional East and West Coast locations have been established since then.

The Wu-Tang Clan is a rap group that formed in the early 1990s.

image that seemed true to himself. At a party during his sophomore year, he put his name into a website designed to generate a stage name in the style of the rap group the Wu-Tang Clan. The system produced the name "Childish Gambino." Glover liked the name so much that it became his musical moniker.

Glover was also part of several sketch comedy groups. He began performing around New York City, including at the famed Upright Citizens Brigade (UCB) Theatre, where he had the opportunity to do improvisational comedy

with well-known comedians. Glover later credited his UCB training with preparing him for his career. During this time, he also had small parts in sketches on *Late Night with Conan O'Brien*.

Glover met two fellow students, DC Pierson and Dominic Dierkes, in a comedy group called the Hammerkatz. The three cofounded a comedy trio called Derrick Comedy and began making videos around campus and posting them to a new video platform called YouTube. Several of the group's videos went viral and caught the attention of entertainment industry insiders. At age 23, Glover was about to catch his big break.

YOUTUBE

YouTube was new territory when Derrick Comedy began making short, low-budget comedy videos and posting them online. The video hosting website's first video was posted on April 23, 2005. The video, "Me at the zoo," showed one of YouTube's founders at the San Diego Zoo. In 2006, Google bought YouTube for $1.65 billion.[8] With millions of views, Derrick Comedy's YouTube videos were some of the first to demonstrate the viral nature of video content. They also helped usher in the era of short-form web comedy.

BIG BREAKS

In 2006, Glover worked as a resident assistant (R.A.) in the campus dorms and volunteered for experiments in the psychology department to make extra money. One day, he received an email from television producer David Miner asking for writing samples. Miner, an executive producer, was looking for writers for a new show called *30 Rock*, which was created by *Saturday Night Live* alum Tina Fey. Miner had heard about Glover through a teacher at UCB and was intrigued by Derrick Comedy's viral videos.

Glover's writing samples included a packet of comedy sketches and a sample screenplay, or spec script, he had written for *The Simpsons*. The material impressed Miner and Fey, who hired Glover as a staff writer for their show. He continued living in the dorms even as he started working on *30 Rock*. Glover graduated from NYU in 2006 with a degree in dramatic writing.

NBC's *30 Rock*, named for the 30 Rockefeller Plaza building in New York, premiered in October of that year. The show parodied the behind-the-scenes happenings

While working on *30 Rock*, Glover occasionally appeared as a performer in the fictional sketch-comedy show that served as the series' premise.

of a live sketch show that closely resembled *SNL*. The comedy landed on many critics' best-of-the-year lists and won an Emmy Award for Outstanding Comedy Series. The show ran through 2013.

Over the next several years, Glover made occasional cameos on *30 Rock* in addition to his writing duties. He also began performing stand-up comedy around New York. In 2007, he auditioned to play presidential candidate Barack Obama on *SNL* during the presidential election season but didn't get the role.

THE KENNETH CONNECTION

Glover surprised some in his writing audition for *30 Rock* when, rather than pitching, or presenting, story ideas for the character played by African American comedian Tracy Morgan, he pitched for the character played by white comedian Jack McBrayer. McBrayer played Kenneth Parcell, a naive and cheerful NBC employee. Glover said that he had more in common with Kenneth than Tracy at the time: "I was a wide-eyed kid, eager to please."[1] As a result, the character of Kenneth shares a hometown with Glover— Stone Mountain, Georgia.

STEPPING INTO THE RAP GAME

Glover enjoyed writing for *30 Rock,* but it didn't leave much time for the other creative endeavors that he wanted to pursue. So when the Writers Guild of America

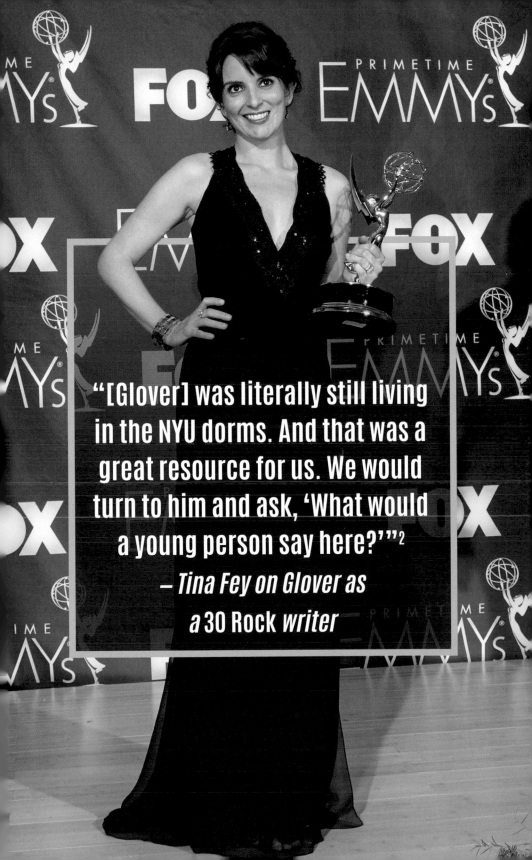

"[Glover] was literally still living in the NYU dorms. And that was a great resource for us. We would turn to him and ask, 'What would a young person say here?'"[2]
— Tina Fey on Glover as a 30 Rock writer

went on strike in late 2007, temporarily halting production on scripted shows such as *30 Rock*, Glover seized the opportunity to create music as Childish Gambino.

In June 2008, he released the rap mixtape *Sick Boi* for free online. Fans and critics whose knowledge of Glover was limited to his viral online comedy videos or his work as a television writer were skeptical upon hearing he was releasing rap tracks, especially under the silly-sounding name. Childish Gambino was still trying to find a delivery that would differentiate himself from other rappers, and the majority of his lyrics did not include the personal subject matter that would resonate in his later projects. Still,

SEARCHING FOR OBAMA

In 2008, *SNL* had a problem to solve—they needed an actor to portray presential candidate Barack Obama in their upcoming sketches. Comedians Jordan Peele of *MADtv* and Jordan Carlos of *The Colbert Report* auditioned in addition to Glover, but the role went to *SNL* cast member Fred Armisen, who is of Japanese and Venezuelan heritage. The decision—and the dark makeup Armisen wore in his portrayal—was widely criticized. One *HuffPost* writer remarked that the show was "apparently unable to find one black comedian able to do an impression of the frontrunner for Most Important Black Person of the 21st Century."[3] Glover joined a string of other comedians who unsuccessfully auditioned for *SNL* but went on to have wildly successful careers, including Steve Carrell, Jim Carrey, Stephen Colbert, Geena Davis, and Kevin Hart.

Childish Gambino caught some attention with his songs, which touched on topics ranging from his stand-up comedy with the UCB ("Naw naw, y'all funny, y'all from UCB?") to his love for hooded sweatshirts ("Got a pouch in the front that holds my CDs/And warms my hands when it's too breezy").[4]

Glover later remembered some of the criticism of *Sick Boi*, saying, "People were asking, 'Why's his voice so high? Why is he rapping about Tina Fey? That's not going to get you any street cred.'"[5] For his part, Glover was still figuring out how to reconcile the stereotypical hip-hop idea of "street cred," or respect, with a product that felt authentic.

> "I think the balance of being, I guess, a good person is actively looking for and through other people's points of view."[6]
> – Donald Glover, 2018

COMMUNITY COMES TOGETHER

Although he found success writing for *30 Rock*—the show won the Writers Guild Award for Outstanding Writing in a Television Comedy Series twice while Glover worked there—Glover was ready for something new. In 2009, he decided to spend more time focusing on his stand-up career and told Fey that he would be moving to Los Angeles. According to Fey, "Usually, when writers tell you they want to pursue performing, you want to tell them to keep their day jobs. But with Donald, I had to agree that his talent, youth, and handsomeness were not to be wasted sitting on my living room floor."[7] It was a risk to leave a paying job, and Glover's Childish Gambino music projects weren't earning him money. But Glover didn't need to worry—after being unemployed for just six days, he was surprised to be cast on another NBC comedy.

Created by Dan Harmon, *Community* centered on a group of misfit students in a Colorado community

WRITERS ON STRIKE

About 12,000 television and film writers went on strike for 100 days between November 2007 and February 2008, forcing most scripted television shows, including *30 Rock*, to stop production. The strike resulted from pay negotiation disagreements between the Writers Guild of America and the Alliance of Motion Picture and Television Producers. One of the writers' demands was to be compensated for their work in what was known as "new media." This pertained to digital and streaming videos, which were relatively new forms of media consumption. At the time, most or all profits were going to large studios. Many actors also joined the demonstrations to show their support. The sides eventually reached an agreement, and the Writers Guild of America members voted to return to work on February 12.

Glover's character on *Community* was known for getting into larger-than-life situations with characters played by Alison Brie, *left,* and Yvette Nicole Brown, *right*.

college. Glover played Troy Barnes, a former football player who embraces his goofy personality. "I auditioned, but I didn't think it was going to go anywhere," Glover said. "I just thought they'd want a good-looking, hunky, football-player-y white dude."[8] The ensemble cast also featured Alison Brie, Yvette Nicole Brown, Chevy Chase, Joel McHale, Ken Jeong, and others.

In 2013, *Community* creator Dan Harmon discussed the show during a panel at an entertainment convention in San Diego, California.

Filmed in Hollywood, California, the first season of *Community* ran from September 2009 to May 2010. The show quickly developed a dedicated fan base for its refreshing format, clever jokes, and talented cast. For his part, Glover earned praise for his breakout performance. "You can feel his potential," said Harmon. "Someday I'll be cashing in on the fact that I worked with him."[9] Critics were likewise smitten, dubbing Glover the "heart of the series" and praising his comedic instincts.[10]

MYSTERY TEAM COMEDY MACHINE

Besides continuing to hone his own stand-up comedy and releasing another mixtape (*Poindexter* in September 2009), Glover was still working with Derrick Comedy. Glover enjoyed the freedom of the comedy group's work compared with the restrictions of Hollywood, saying, "We do whatever we want without worrying about standards and practices or money."[11]

In 2008, Derrick Comedy took a break from making online sketch videos to work on its biggest project yet: a full-length film. Titled *Mystery Team*, the film was a spoof of children's detective stories and featured a group of teens working to solve a murder. The film was independently made, which meant it was not supported by a major studio. The Derrick Comedy members funded the project

FILM DEBUTS

Derrick Comedy's *Mystery Team* movie served as the film debut of actors who would become well known in their field. The cast included Aubrey Plaza (*Parks and Recreation*), Ellie Kemper (*The Office*, *Unbreakable Kimmy Schmidt*), Ben Schwartz (*Parks and Recreation*), and Bobby Moynihan (*SNL*). The movie was filmed mainly in New Hampshire, the hometown of fellow NYU grads Dan Ecker and Meggie McFadden, who served as the group's director and producer, respectively.

The cast of *Mystery Team* posed for photos at the 2009 Sundance Film Festival.

through earnings from their YouTube videos and online commercials they produced. In addition to cowriting, producing, and scoring the film, Glover also starred in it.

In 2009, the film premiered at the Sundance Film Festival in Utah, the largest such festival in the United States. It received mixed reviews from critics.

The *Los Angeles Times* described it as a "charming effort," and *The Boston Globe* said it was "a deeply dumb movie made by pretty smart people."[12] Still, many reviewers said the comedy group had potential. The members later secured the film's limited release in theaters, the locations of which were dictated by fans voting online.

Chapter Four

SUPERHEROES AND MIXTAPES

Glover's fame increased as he continued juggling rapping, DJing, and writing in comedy alongside his acting job on *Community*, and he gained a diverse fan following for his different projects. Now that he was creating music, he couldn't seem to stop. In January 2010, he released *I Am Just a Rapper*, a mixtape that captured wider attention and signaled that Childish Gambino was a rapper to watch.

Unlike his previous two mixtapes, Glover did not produce every track on *I Am Just a Rapper* by himself. Each of the mixtape's seven tracks featured him rapping over samples, which are parts of other artists' songs. The sampled songs came from indie artists including Animal Collective, Grizzly Bear, and Sleigh Bells. The mixtape was followed a month later by *I Am Just a Rapper 2*.

Childish Gambino began performing at venues across the United States after releasing two mixtapes and an extended play (EP) in just over one year.

Soon after, Glover showcased his stand-up skills in a half-hour set on the TV show *Comedy Central Presents*. He continued performing stand-up in New York and Los Angeles. Also in 2010, 26-year-old Glover won the Rising Comedy Star of the Year Award at Montreal's Just for Laughs Comedy Festival, where he performed music as Childish Gambino. Additionally, he voiced a character on an episode of the popular stop-motion sketch comedy show *Robot Chicken*.

That summer, Glover was at the center of a buzz around a completely different genre—superhero movies. Following an article on the tech website Gizmodo that suggested the newest version of Spider-Man be played by an actor of color, a fan commented that Glover would be the perfect fit. Glover joined the discussion through Twitter and

KEEPING BUSY

The people who surrounded Glover often commented on his busy schedule. His days are always filled keeping up with his various projects. A 2011 profile of Glover in *The Village Voice*, titled "Donald Glover Is More Talented Than You," offered a sample of his exhausting schedule. Within a few days, he released an EP; gave interviews as Childish Gambino; shot scenes for *Community*; wrote, mixed, and posted songs; and prepared for comedy and music performances.

began campaigning to get an audition. Internet users determined to make it happen answered his call. Using the hashtag "#Donald4SpiderMan," the campaign went viral.[1] Stan Lee, the creator of *Spider-Man*, even contributed to the discussion, diplomatically saying that anyone should have a chance to audition. Glover was "floored" by the response, saying, "The amount of support and people emailing me, calling me—I think that's really cool that people have that much faith in me."[2] However, Glover wasn't asked to audition, and the role went to actor Andrew Garfield.

> "He is equally engaging whether he is dropping rhymes, doing stand-up, or acting. . . . Donald holds one of my favorite qualities as an artist—he's an original."[3]
> – Director Jason Reitman, 2010

CULDESAC CATCHES ATTENTION

As he gained recognition as a multitalented performer, Glover had more demands than ever on his time. Although he was being pulled in countless directions, Glover took to heart the advice of his *Community* costars Alison Brie and Gillian Jacobs, who encouraged him to follow through with his rap aspirations. "That changed everything," Glover remembered. "I just said, 'I'll do whatever I want.'"[4] And what he wanted to do was complete another rap project.

In July 2010, Childish Gambino released *Culdesac*, a mixtape that he distributed for free on the internet. The mixtape contained 16 tracks and featured samples from artists such as Adele and Diana Ross. After his years of grinding away at his craft, Childish Gambino had hit upon a sound and flow that best showcased his artistic talents.

"I don't see a limit for me. I want to do everything."[5]
— Donald Glover, 2011

For this newest project, Glover collaborated with Ludwig Göransson, the Swedish composer who worked on *Community*. Göransson engineered and coproduced tracks on the mixtape, most of which Glover recorded inside his trailer between shooting scenes for the show.

The mixtape earned largely positive reviews from critics and fans, particularly for its production, beats, and Glover's refusal to pigeon-hole himself into a stereotypical rap sound. Some reviewers compared Glover to hip-hop legend Tupac Shakur. An article on *HuffPost* said, "It becomes clear from listening to *Culdesac* that Glover thinks he's on the highest creative level possible, a la

Tupac, and maybe in his own way he is."[6] It seemed as though Childish Gambino was finally being taken seriously—and rapping had officially become more than a side project.

IAMDONALD TOUR

Glover's frantic pace continued the following year. In March 2011, Childish Gambino released his first extended play record (EP), titled *EP*, for free digital download. Featuring five tracks, *EP* was written and produced by Childish Gambino and Göransson. The music video for the track "Freaks and Geeks" gained viral traction online, leading MTV.com to post, "If you don't know who Donald Glover is yet, start paying attention."[7]

STEPHEN GLOVER

Although the brothers often collaborate, Stephen Glover has tried to avoid the stigma of being known as Childish Gambino's little brother and proved himself to be an accomplished creator in his own right. Stephen began making music at age 17 and released his first rap mixtape, *Frequent Flyer LP*, in 2011. He is often credited as "Steve G. Lover" in his performances. In recent years, critics have noted the distinctions between the brothers' hip-hop styles, such as the pronounced Atlanta rap influence in Stephen's sound. Stephen became an important part of his brother's creative circle and went on to win screenwriting awards for his contributions in the brothers' later television work.

Shortly after releasing *EP*, Childish Gambino appeared at an MTV party in Austin, Texas.

Outsiders may have wondered how Glover could keep up with the simultaneous projects, shoots, and performances. Despite people around him—including his mother and his manager—telling him to slow down, Glover refused to go any less than full steam ahead. That often meant he focused on his next big project rather than his personal life, about which he was notoriously tight-lipped. He subsisted on little sleep, remarking, "I have so many ideas and things I want to do, sleeping isn't going to accomplish that."[8]

Glover had another project in the works and began a 25-city nationwide tour in April 2011. The IAMDONALD tour was a one-man show that featured Glover's stand-up comedy and video sketches, as well as a Childish Gambino rap concert. Glover told media outlets that he took his cue from the Disney Channel show *Hannah Montana* for insight into how to entertain audiences as both a musician and actor. Although the tour was successful, Glover decided afterward to take a step back from combining the mediums of stand-up comedy and music, instead focusing on the crafts individually for the time being.

CHILDISH GAMBINO AT BONNAROO

In June 2011, Glover performed a comedy set as himself as well as a music set as Childish Gambino at the annual Bonnaroo Music and Arts Festival in Manchester, Tennessee. His rap performance was praised in *Spin* magazine: "Backed by a five-piece funk-rock band, Glover pogo'd around the stage in his Garth Brooks t-shirt and skinny black shorts . . . with joyous abandon."[9] Eminem, Arcade Fire, Widespread Panic, the Black Keys, and Buffalo Springfield led the long list of performers at that year's festival. In 2019, Childish Gambino's name would be one of the featured top names in the festival lineup.

Childish Gambino performed at the 2011 Bonnaroo Music and Arts Festival as part of the IAMDONALD tour.

In late August, Glover signed with Glassnote Records. It was a move that surprised some who weren't familiar with Glover's wide-ranging appreciation for different types of music, as the record label was known for producing indie and alternative records. But true to form, Glover wasn't interested in doing the expected. The label was confident that Childish Gambino would fit right in as a progressive, alternative performer. Glover hoped the new deal would position him for success.

GLASSNOTE RECORDS

Glassnote Records, founded by music executive Daniel Glass in 2007, represents many of the music scene's most successful indie and alternative artists. It was named "Best Indie Label" in a 2011 issue of Rolling Stone. Its clients have included Chvrches, Mumford & Sons, Phoenix, and Secondhand Serenade. Before signing Childish Gambino, the label had been impressed with the artist's progressive online presence, his interactions with fans, and his practice of making his music available for free. "He knows his audience," commented Glass.[10]

RISING STAR

In November 2011, Childish Gambino released his debut studio album, *Camp*, with Glassnote Records. The album's debut single, "Bonfire," had been released two months prior. The album sold 52,000 copies in its first week and debuted at Number 11 on the *Billboard* 200. The track "Heartbeat" reached Number 54 on *Billboard*'s Hot R&B/Hip-Hop Songs chart.

While some critics praised Childish Gambino's humor, emotional depth, and inclusion of topics such as race and masculinity on the album, others called his delivery "cartoonish" and "self-obsessed" and questioned the rapper's portrayal of himself as an outsider.[1] One major criticism of the *Camp* album was the perceived objectification of women in Childish Gambino's latest tracks. "Glover's performance as Gambino is purposefully over the top," wrote Michael P. Jeffries in the *Atlantic*, "but comedic license does not excuse the sexism in his lyrics."[2] This criticism would continue to plague Childish Gambino's later work, with critics pointing out that

Childish Gambino's 2012 tour helped show people that he was a serious musical artist, not just an actor who occasionally rapped.

"AIN'T HOOD ENOUGH"

In *Camp*, Childish Gambino tackled race and personal identity in tracks such as "Hold You Down," in which he rapped, "Culture shock at barber shops 'cause I ain't hood enough / We all look the same to the cops, ain't that good enough? / The black experience is blackened serious / 'Cause being black, my experience, is no one hearin' us."[4] In the track "Fire Fly," he focused on how he didn't fit the stereotypical mold of a hip-hop artist.

> "We expected better than your run-of-the-mill misogyny from someone like Glover."[5]
> – *Caroline Pate*, Bustle, 2013

he reduced women in songs to objects or status symbols—in effect, critics said, Childish Gambino was adhering to stereotypical hip-hop practices even as he supposedly rejected them.

In *Time* magazine, Claire Suddath opined that the album lacked a clear theme, perhaps because its creator was similarly complex. "He acts, he writes, he still does stand-up, and yes, he also raps," she wrote. "Some people can't be put into a box that easily."[3] Indeed, the same month that *Camp* came out, Comedy Central aired Glover's first hour-long comedy special, *Weirdo*, with material ranging from the failed Spider-Man campaign to Home Depot to fame to racism. The show had been filmed at New

York City's Union Square Theatre in front of two sold-out crowds. Around the same time, Glover could be spotted making a cameo in the hit feature film *The Muppets*, starring Amy Adams and Jason Segel.

CAMP GAMBINO

Following a month-long delay due to a broken foot, Childish Gambino's nationwide Camp Gambino tour kicked off in April 2012. Childish Gambino continued convincing audiences of his authenticity as a musical artist, with Jeff Niesel of *Scene* magazine reporting after a Cleveland, Ohio, performance, "Glover's enthusiasm never waned, suggesting his commitment to hip-hop career is more than just a passing fancy."[6]

DONALD'S PLAYLIST

In May 2011, Glover was a guest DJ on California's KCRW radio station. During the show, Glover chose five tracks that influenced him in various ways. The first was "Tell Me a Story" by Nedelle. The second was "I Wish" by Skee-Lo. Glover said, "The thing that I liked about Skee-Lo and I found out later on that I liked about Pharrell [Williams] and stuff like that is that they didn't fit into a box of what a black kid had to be, which I hadn't seen a lot." The third song was "Isobel" by Björk; the fourth was "Something You Forgot" by Lil Wayne. The final song was "A/B Machines" by Sleigh Bells. Glover said, "Number one, it was fun. That was the thing. I feel a lot of people forget how much fun stuff is supposed to be."[7]

In 2012, Childish Gambino performed at the Coachella Valley Music and Arts Festival in Indio, California.

A few months later, Childish Gambino's sixth mixtape, *Royalty*, was released as a free digital download. The tracks featured an impressive array of big-name guests, including hip-hop artists Chance the Rapper, Nipsey Hussle, Ghostface Killah, and ScHoolboy Q, in addition to Glover's *30 Rock* mentor Tina Fey, musical artist Beck, NBA star Blake Griffin, Wu-Tang Clan member RZA, and Glover's brother Stephen (as Steve G. Lover III).

The mixtape's diverse sampling included hooks from pop star Britney Spears as well as French electronic artist Kavinsky. Corban Goble of *Stereogum*, who had criticized *Camp*, noted that the mixtape had a "surprising amount of quality and variety for a free mixtape."[8] Meanwhile, Childish Gambino released additional songs and also collaborated with British singer Leona Lewis, rapping on her song "Trouble." The track reached Number 4 on the UK Singles Chart.

A RAPPER ON TV

Early in 2013, Glover was nominated for a National Association for the Advancement of Colored People (NAACP) Image Award for his work on *Community*. The annual awards honor outstanding performances in film, television, music,

FORGET ABOUT IT

As a musical artist, Glover had to start from somewhere. But he has since disowned at least some of his early work, including his first Childish Gambino mixtape, *The Younger I Get* (2002). In a 2011 *Spin* profile, Glover likened the mixtape's unpolished vocals to a "decrepit Drake." He was serious about distancing himself from the mixtape—and keeping it out of the hands of listeners who were eager to hear his early tracks as his fame grew. "It does surprise me in this internet age that it hasn't surfaced *anywhere*," said Glover's NYU classmate and collaborator Chaz Kangas, "but perhaps that's more of a testament to how those of us who have it respect Donald's wishes and haven't leaked it."[9]

and literature. The same year, Glover made an appearance in the feature film *The To Do List* alongside Aubrey Plaza. More talked about, however, was his two-episode arc in the second season of HBO's hit comedy-drama *Girls*, which stirred discussions about race.

On *Girls*, Glover portrayed the boyfriend of the character Hannah, played by the show's creator, Lena Dunham. The show's first season had been criticized for its lack of racial diversity, and some speculated that Glover's brief stint on the show was meant to appease critics. Although Dunham stated that Glover was cast because of his talents and not his race, she apologized to Glover if he had felt the show tokenized him as an African American man. Glover reportedly responded, "Let's not think back on mistakes we made in the past, let's just focus on what lies in front of us."[10]

Also on the television front, Glover signed with the TV network FX to write, produce, and star in a show called *Atlanta*, billed at the time as a "music-themed comedy."[11] Glover had unsuccessfully pitched the show to several other networks before he landed on FX. The network was willing to accommodate his Childish Gambino touring schedule and other projects.

RACISM ON SET

Even as a breakout star of *Community*, Glover experienced racist comments from one of his own costars, famous comedian Chevy Chase. In one instance, Chase, who was known for being difficult on set, told Glover that people thought he was funnier because he was black. In another incident, production stopped after Chase used a racial slur. Creator Dan Harmon apologized to Glover for Chase's behavior, later saying, "Chevy was the first to realize how immensely gifted Donald was, and the way he expressed his jealousy was to try to throw Donald off." For his part, Glover didn't let it bother him, viewing Chase as an icon who was past his prime. "A true artist has to be ok with his reign being over," Glover remarked.[12]

BECAUSE THE INTERNET

Meanwhile, Childish Gambino was hard at work on what was arguably his most ambitious project to date. In August 2013, he released his second studio album, again with Glassnote Records. The album, titled *Because the Internet*, debuted at Number 7 on the *Billboard 200* chart and included popular tracks such as "Crawl" and "Sweatpants."

Fitting with the album's title, Glover utilized the internet to create additional layers of fan interaction with the project. He included special content and hidden files on his website and partnered with other websites to host live fan events. Coinciding with the release, Childish Gambino released a 72-page screenplay designed to be read while listening to the album. He also wrote and starred in a 25-minute short film, *Clapping for the Wrong Reasons*, directed by Hiro Murai, who later directed the video for "This is America." Fans immediately set to work interpreting the works, seeking to uncover connections and callbacks to other Childish Gambino projects. When Glover shared confessional notes on his Instagram page that referenced depression and loneliness, some fans were concerned about his well-being, while others believed the posts were promoting the theme of his album.

The album received generally positive reviews, with many critics grading it a marked improvement from his debut album. The track "3005" was met with particular acclaim as critics remarked on Childish Gambino's wit, vision, and hooks as well as his commentary on the

GETTING TO *SESAME STREET*

In 2013, Glover visited *Sesame Street* for an episode of the show's forty-third season. Glover played a fictional famous rapper named LMNOP (a parody of musical group LMFAO). Sporting an afro, bright orange vest, purple glasses, and green headband, Glover strummed a homemade instrument in front of a crowd of dancing kids, parents, and Muppets. In a song about solving problems, he sang, "Don't run around in circles, don't scream and shout/Just put your heads together and figure it out."[13]

> "I don't call myself anything. I've spent most of my life being labeled and I've learned that really doesn't help anyone."[17]
>
> – Childish Gambino

internet age. With some exceptions, even reviewers who had problems with the album credited its creativity. According to reviewer Killian Fox in the *Observer*, who ranked the album three out of five stars,

> Glover reflects on some unsettling phenomena of our internet-addled age, such as the 3D printing of guns—and his restless delivery . . . is matched by jerky, off-kilter production. The results are intriguing, occasionally frustrating, [and] rarely boring.[14]

Grantland's Zach Dionne said the album's "capable adventurousness is gripping."[15] The album was later certified gold, a designation by the Recording Industry Association of American (RIAA) that certifies it sold 500,000 units.[16] Units include album sales, track sales, and track streams. The album reached Number 1 on *Billboard*'s Top Rap Albums chart.

Glover's ongoing work on various projects continued to be fodder for media commentary. He was described as a "restless polyglot" by Craig Jenkins of *Pitchfork*, who added, "You can watch him tire of a medium just as he

During some shows, Childish Gambino plays instruments, including the piano.

appears to get good at it."[18] As Childish Gambino set out on his 2014 Deep Web Tour, which included London, Paris, and other European cities in addition to US stops, the artist didn't seem to know any other way. He was determined to do it all.

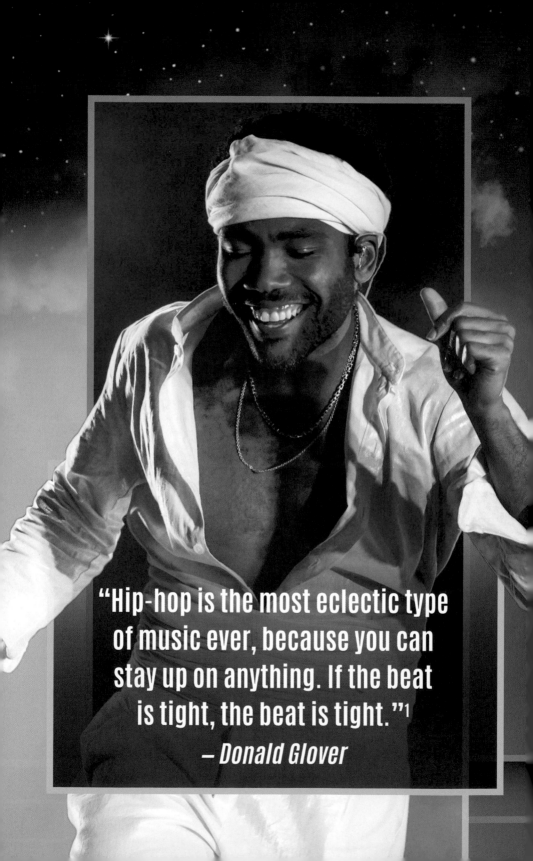

"Hip-hop is the most eclectic type of music ever, because you can stay up on anything. If the beat is tight, the beat is tight."[1]
– *Donald Glover*

ON TO THE NEXT

With other projects on the horizon, Glover decided that after four seasons his time on *Community* was up. "I'm glad things end because it forces things to progress," he said at one point.[2] His departure appeared timely, as the show had been weighed down by various disputes between members of the cast, producers, and studio that culminated with the exits of other members of the cast and crew. Fans and critics noted that the sitcom that had once been seen as revolutionary to the genre was now floundering.

Community's creator, Dan Harmon, had recently returned to the show and convinced Glover to stay on as a guest star for the first handful of episodes of season five to satisfactorily wrap up his character's storyline. The fifth episode of the season, "Geothermal Escapism," aired in early 2014 and marked Glover's last episode. He was already on to the next project.

Glover left *Community* to focus on his rap career as Childish Gambino.

Community fans were sad to see Glover go because they enjoyed his character's scenes with Abed, played by Danny Pudi, *right*.

RACE COMMENTARY

After more than a decade honing his rap skills, Childish Gambino had built self-confidence in his craft and message. "I feel like I'm entering a point where it's like,

'I understand what I'm doing,'"[3] he remarked. Tied closely
to that feeling was Glover's continued social commentary
about race in America, which he shared not only through
his Childish Gambino tracks but also his Twitter account.

In August 2014, race relations in the United States came to a head when unarmed African American teenager Michael Brown was shot and killed by a police officer in Ferguson, Missouri. The incident sparked riots and a national debate on police brutality and race in America. A few days later, Glover posted a poem through a series of tweets, which people took to have been inspired by the shooting.

"I feel like our job as young blacks in this country is to show our worth. Cause right now they view us as worthless."[6]
— Donald Glover, 2014

In the poem, Glover wrote about white privilege and how he believed African American males are judged. He later tweeted in further explanation: "i want people to understand i wasn't under any influence last night. after hearing a friend sobbing and after talking with my mom, i wrote that poem."[4] He also tweeted that police should have to wear recording devices, saying that he had been threatened by police twice in the past year despite his celebrity status, "so when someone calls me a white rapper, i wanna make sure they understand i don't have all the benefits."[5] Glover later erased the content from his social media accounts and stated that the internet made him feel less human.

NEW TRACKS

Childish Gambino's artistic assuredness carried through onto his next project. In October 2014, he released his seventh mixtape, the 11-song *STN MTN* (an abbreviation for his hometown of Stone Mountain), for free online. The next day, he released a seven-song EP called *Kauai*

through Glassnote Records, which hit Number 1 on the *Billboard* Top Rap Album chart. When Childish Gambino had previously released the EP's first single, "Sober," the music video had racked up more than five million views within a month of release.[7]

The combined mixtape/EP project (known as *STN MTN / Kauai*) was seen as a concept album, which is a collection of tracks that have a collective purpose or meaning.

While *STN MTN* referenced Atlanta hip-hop ("I had a dream I ran Atlanta, and I was on every radio station"), the softer-toned *Kauai* was based on the Hawaiian island of Kauai ("It looked like we were just floating in an abyss/ Honestly, when I see her face I just smile I guess").[8]

SECRET TRACK

In 2014, a savvy internet fan uncovered a secret remix of Childish Gambino's "3005" track. Childish Gambino had previously alluded to a secret track and dropped clues in the promotional screenplay for his *Because the Internet* album. After Childish Gambino released his *STN MTN / Kauai* project, the internet user put together the clues to discover a hidden file on Childish Gambino's website—an a cappella track. When the user played the vocals over *STN MTN*'s final song "3005 (Beach Picnic Version)," it created the new track. Childish Gambino confirmed the discovery by retweeting the user's explanation that had been posted online.

Childish Gambino reported that half the proceeds from *Kauai* would go toward changing policies regarding police body cameras. The other half would benefit the Hawaiian island. Some reviewers took the album's dual nature to represent the artist's divided life as both Donald Glover and Childish Gambino.

The overall reception to Childish Gambino was also divided. Writing for *Consequence of Sound*, reviewer Michael Madden wrote, "Depending on

FEELING HIMSELF

At a 2014 performance in Sydney, Australia, Childish Gambino stirred things up by calling out other hip-hop artists by name, including Kendrick Lamar, Drake, and SCHoolboy Q. "I'm the best rapper, definitely top 5," he rapped. Childish Gambino stood by his comments later that month, saying that every rapper should feel as though they are the best. He said he called out those rappers in particular because he saw them as the ones to beat. "When [other artists are] good, I'm like, 'Man, I wish I had done that,'" he said. "It's competition."[10]

"Glover's career speaks of a man that shatters most stereotypes closely associated with blackness especially those tightly interwoven into rap music."[11]

– H. Drew Blackman, Consequence of Sound, 2014

who you ask, he's one of hip-hop's smartest MCs or a short-shorts-wearing outsider who's unable to see why he's unwelcome." Madden added that the rapper's improved work was "producing more applause and fewer face-palms."[9]

Although some people still criticized his work, Childish Gambino was continuing to win over audiences for his provocative, clever commentary—and he was beginning to receive industry recognition as well. In December 2014, Childish Gambino earned two Grammy nominations for Because the Internet: Best Rap Album and Best Rap Performance for the song "3005." Although Glover was humble about the nominations, he admitted that having the phrase "Grammy-nominated" in front of his name would lend more credibility to his future work. "It means . . . when I do a film and do my own music to it, it's not like a vanity project," he said.[12] The awards went to rappers Eminem and Kendrick Lamar, respectively.

GLOVER AT THE MOVIES

Throughout 2014 and 2015, Glover took on supporting roles in a handful of feature films. First, he appeared in the Disney family comedy *Alexander and the Terrible, Horrible, No Good, Very Bad Day*, which starred Steve Carrell and Jennifer Garner. Next, the sci-fi horror film *The Lazarus Effect* featured Glover as a scientist who helps bring

ROSCOE'S WETSUIT

Fans of Childish Gambino have noticed clues, patterns, and hidden meanings within his albums and uncovered connections to past projects and storylines. At one point, the phrase "roscoe's wetsuit" (mentioned throughout the *Because the Internet* screenplay) began trending after Glover tweeted the words. Some fans speculated that the phrase could be a future album, collaboration, or clue, while others believed it was Glover's way of demonstrating that people share things on the internet because everyone else is doing it, thereby creating meaning from nothing—in short, things exist simply "because the internet."[13]

Göransson won three Grammy awards in 2019, two of which were for his work on Childish Gambino's song "This Is America."

a person back to life. Then, in the Channing Tatum–led box-office hit *Magic Mike XXL*, Glover played a rapper/singer. His character's cover of a Bruno Mars song was included on the film's soundtrack. Finally, Glover played a scientist involved in a space rescue mission in the sci-fi film *The Martian*. Starring Matt Damon, *The Martian* received widespread recognition, including seven Oscar nominations. Also in 2015, Glover finally got the chance to play Spider-Man. He voiced the title character in Disney XD's "Ultimate Spider-Man" animated series. The show followed the adventures of teenager Miles Morales, who took on the superhero role from Peter Parker.

In November, Childish Gambino could be heard on the soundtrack for the film *Creed*, the seventh installment in the Rocky boxing film franchise. Childish Gambino's frequent collaborator Göransson composed the film's score, which included the track "Waiting for My Moment," performed by Childish Gambino, Jhené Aiko, and Vince Staples.

At the end of 2015, Glover received exciting news when FX ordered a ten-episode season of his television show *Atlanta*. "*Atlanta* draws on Donald's considerable talents as a musician, actor, and writer to give us something unique," announced FX president of original programming Nick Grad.[14] Heading up a show on a major network meant Glover would be adding a whole new skill set to his resume—and it could be the biggest career opportunity of his life.

WELCOME TO ATLANTA

On September 6, 2016, *Atlanta* premiered on FX. The first half-hour episode, "The Big Bang," was written by Glover and directed by Murai. The show followed Glover's character, Earnest "Earn" Marks, who returns to his hometown of Atlanta broke and begins managing his cousin, a fledgling rapper named Paper Boi, who is played by Brian Tyree Henry.

In creating the show, Glover put all of his effort into making the ten episodes iconic. Glover referred to the TV shows of African American comedians Bernie Mac and Dave Chapelle for inspiration, noting them for their honesty as well as their comedy. The approach paid off, and the response was overwhelmingly positive. *Atlanta* received the highest ratings for a basic cable comedy in years.

Glover's acting in *Atlanta* received praise from both fans and critics.

The series continued to earn praise over its ten-episode first season. Critics lauded its creativity, experimentation, and multidimensional characters. The *Atlantic* described it as "gloriously unpredictable" and the *Guardian* called it "what television looks like when writers and creative teams are allowed to take risks."[1] By its season finale, *Atlanta* had become the most-watched comedy in the history of FX, pulling in an average of more than five million viewers an episode.[2]

BACKED BY ROYALTY

Although Glover was the mastermind behind *Atlanta*, he hadn't done it alone. The show's writing team was

TROJAN HORSE

Although FX initially billed *Atlanta* as a half-hour comedy about the city's music industry, viewers and critics quickly realized upon its premiere that the show was more complex than they had been led to believe. According to Glover, that misdirection had been intentional. "I was Trojan-horsing FX," he said later, adding that he had kept details about the show vague on purpose. "If I told them what I really wanted to do, it wouldn't have gotten made."[3]

"I think directing is like everything else; if you're storytelling, then you have to be really confident in what you're telling."[4]
  – *Donald Glover, 2017*

made up entirely of African American writers—a rarity in Hollywood. "It wasn't a conscious decision, really," Glover said. "I knew I wanted people with similar experiences who understood the language and the mindset of the characters and their environment."[5]

For their efforts, the team behind *Atlanta* captured two Emmy awards out of its six nominations: Outstanding Directing for a Comedy Series (Glover) and Outstanding Lead Actor for a Comedy Series (Glover). The former was the first time an African American had won the award and the latter was the first time an African American man had won the award since 1985. Among other honors, Glover also won for Best Actor in a Comedy Series at the Golden Globes.

Glover knew the value of having a reliable team behind him. Over the years, he had surrounded himself with a core group of trusted creative partners. This included his brother,

INSIDE THE WRITERS' ROOM

Some of the writers on *Atlanta* had not worked on a television writing team before. Glover's experiences with *30 Rock* and other shows helped guide the group. "He showed us the ropes of character development and story structure and took the leadership role in the room, and then we just let the ideas out," said Fam Udeorji, a writer on *Atlanta* and one-half of Glover's management team.[6]

In 2016, Glover won a Critics' Choice award for his role on *Atlanta*.

Stephen, who was also a writer on *Atlanta*. It also included the other musicians and artists who helped build Glover's career and everything that went along with it, from albums and marketing to tours and websites. Glover called the group Royalty. This was a nod to the 2012 Childish Gambino mixtape that brought many of them together.

That circle of support became increasingly important as the number of opportunities grew and the acclaim of *Atlanta* cemented his star status. As Glover continued finding success, he realized he wouldn't be able to please everyone. But, even more empowering, he had no interest in doing so.

A SOUL AWAKENING

For his next album, Glover wanted to connect with his fans in a new way. He explained to his Royalty team that he wanted to host an immersive, multiday performance and camping event in the desert to release his new Childish Gambino tracks. The music would be paired with amazing storytelling visuals. He called the event Pharos, after the name of ancient Egypt's Lighthouse of Alexandria, one of the seven wonders of the ancient world. The three-day, six-show concert event took place inside a giant dome in Joshua Tree, California, and gave fans an exclusive introduction to his new music.

DESERT LIGHTS

It required new heights of creativity, innovation, and technology to make Glover's vision for the Pharos event in Joshua Tree a reality. For the high-tech, computer-generated visuals inside the dome, Glover enlisted the experts at Microsoft, who used sensor technology to capture his movements and translate them into onscreen animation. Glover also had a plan for ensuring that the audience members soaked up the experience without distraction—no phones were allowed. All attendees had to agree to turn over their phones upon entry to be locked away during the concert.

Listeners were treated to a whole new sound when Childish Gambino's third studio album, *"Awaken, My Love!"*, dropped on December 2, 2016, through Glassnote Records. The 1970s funk and sultry R&B vibes were a striking departure from Childish Gambino's previous rap offerings and offered a new dimension of soul along with high-pitched vocals and mesmerizing instrumentals. The vinyl release of *"Awaken, My Love!"* also included a virtual reality (VR) headset and app with access to VR live performances, including the Pharos event.

The album sold 72,000 copies in the first week and debuted at Number 1 on *Billboard*'s R&B charts. Critics widely acclaimed the album, particularly the track "Redbone," which was streamed 8.4 million times within the week.[7] It peaked

GET OUT

"Redbone" was featured in the opening credits of the 2017 film *Get Out*, a horror movie about the experience of being black in America. Nominated for four Oscars and winning one for Best Original Screenplay, the chilling film was the breakout directing debut of comedian Jordan Peele, then best known for costarring in the sketch comedy show *Key & Peele*. The song's lyrics ("Gon' catch you sleepin' / Now stay woke") resonated with Peele, who said that he was a huge fan of Childish Gambino.[8] Some viewers later saw links between the film and Childish Gambino's 2018 music video "This Is America."

at Number 12 on the Hot 100 chart and was later certified quadruple-platinum.

The album went on to receive five Grammy nominations, including Album of the Year and Record of the Year ("Redbone"). Childish Gambino took home the first Grammy of his career when "Redbone" won for Best Traditional R&B Performance. "It feels pretty surreal," he said in a backstage interview.[9]

OPPORTUNITIES AND ENDINGS

Glover had a string of new projects on the horizon. Earlier in 2016, it was announced that he had landed a role in one of the most popular franchises in history—Star Wars. Glover would play his childhood hero, Lando Calrissian, in an upcoming spin-off movie. In January 2017, Glover signed an exclusive deal with FX to develop new projects. That summer, seven years after his social media campaign to become the new Spider-Man, he appeared in *Spider-Man: Homecoming* as the uncle of Miles Morales. Then it was announced that Glover would

"This idea that the only thing stopping you is your own imagination—that's beautiful, but you still need structure, you still need boundaries, even if you're making them yourself."[10]
— Donald Glover, 2017

Glover played Lando Calrissian in the 2018 movie
Solo: A Star Wars Story.

voice Simba in the 2019 live-action remake of *The Lion King*. All the high-profile projects led *Complex* to wonder, "Have we ever seen an all-encompassing pop-culture wave quite like Donald Glover's?"[11]

Glover also had changes happening in his personal life. In 2017, he revealed that he had become a father the previous year and that fatherhood had influenced the sound of his most recent album. Although Glover was known for being very private about his personal life, he later shared that his partner's name was Michelle

White and their son was named Legend. In his Emmy acceptance speech for *Atlanta*, he thanked White before announcing that they were expecting a second son. Glover's demanding schedule meant that he wasn't able to spend as much time with Legend as he would like, but he explained that it was "because I want to give him everything."[12]

Glover's music fans were abuzz in June 2017 when he announced during a performance that his next Childish Gambino album would be his last. When later pressed for explanation, Glover stood by his declaration. "There's nothing [worse] than like a third sequel, . . . and we're like, 'Again?'"[13] In the same way he had embraced endings throughout his career, Glover viewed the end of Childish Gambino as a necessary means to move forward to bigger and better things.

MOST INFLUENTIAL

In 2017, Glover was named to the "*Time* 100," the magazine's annual list of the 100 most influential people in the world. Glover's *30 Rock* mentor Tina Fey wrote the magazine's feature on him and lauded his drive to succeed in multiple industries. "Now Donald is serving you best-case-scenario millennial realness," she wrote. "He embodies his generation's belief that people can be whatever they want and change what it is they want, at any time."[14] The list also included world leaders, businesspeople, media personalities, athletes, and other celebrities.

THE YEAR OF DONALD

The year 2018 proved to be memorable for Glover on multiple fronts. Hip-hop fans unsure of the future of Childish Gambino's career hoped that more music was on the way when he announced in January that he had signed with RCA Records, which he called a needed change. It was also in January that Glover and White announced the birth of their second son. In March, the much-anticipated second season of *Atlanta* premiered.

Atlanta's writers, cast, and crew weren't immune to the pressures that came along with the surprise acclaim of the first season. Glover in particular felt a need to prove that the accolades were earned. "A lot of this season is me proving to people that I didn't get those Emmys just because of affirmative action" he said.[1] The team decided one way to do that was to make the second season different enough from the first so the two didn't compete.

Glover posed with Chewbacca while promoting *Solo: A Star Wars Story*.

Much as he did for other projects, Glover also paid attention to the audience response on social media.

Titled "Robbin' Season," the second season was darker in tone and named for the time period during the holiday season when robbery rates increase. "It's a tense and desperate time," Stephen said. "We wanted it to be a metaphor for our characters."[2] The show's second round was a smash. The season premiere captured 1.8 million viewers and the series earned 16 Emmy nominations.[3] It took home three of the awards.

STAR POWER

In May, *Solo: A Star Wars Story* premiered in theaters, featuring Glover as the smooth-talking pilot Lando Calrissian. Despite various production delays, Glover enjoyed the experience of filming. Particularly special to Glover was bringing his father, also a Star Wars fan, to see the elaborate film set on the Canary Islands.

The film wasn't a blockbuster but Glover's performance was singled out for praise by critics. The *London Evening Standard* declared, "Donald Glover is the real star of this prequel," and *Vulture* called him "by far the best thing in this film."[5] The film's director, Ron Howard, commended Glover's focus, commitment, and passion for the character.

With his star power rising, Glover seemed to be operating on an entirely different plane as he reached for new creative heights. As he looked to the future, he told the *New Yorker* that he wasn't sure

LANDING LANDO

When Glover first heard rumors of an upcoming film featuring the Star Wars character Lando Calrissian, he knew he had to throw his hat in the ring for the role. When his agent told him the chances of getting the part would be slim, it only further convinced Glover that he could do it. "That was exactly what I needed to . . . . I'm the person who's not supposed to make it, so much so that I don't think people recognize where I came from and what I've done." As a result, Glover studied up on the movies and prepared all he could before the audition. "I killed it, because I was ready."[6]

"He looked like us and talked like us, and seemed to be speaking for a segment of young people who were geeky and quirky and mostly ignored. We loved him for it."[7]

— *Bijan Stephen*, Esquire, *2018*

what lay ahead. "The thing I imagine myself being in the future doesn't exist yet. . . . It's something different and more, something involving fairness and restoring a sense of honor."[8] One thing was for sure—his next project was about to cause the biggest stir yet.

WAKING UP AMERICA

On May 5, Childish Gambino premiered his new track, "This Is America," on *SNL* at the same time the Murai-directed music video dropped on YouTube. Within four days, the video had been viewed 50 million times.[9] As quickly as it collected views, the video spurred opinions, explanations, and rebukes—as well as immediate re-watches to catch details in the chaotic background. Some viewers admired it as a powerful

SYMBOLS OF VIOLENCE

Much of the imagery in the "This Is America" music video revolved around violence and guns, which viewers closely analyzed for symbols and meanings. For example, figures in the video treat guns carefully and wrap them in cloth. Viewers pointed out that the guns were treated with more respect than the people, which some took to be a commentary suggesting that Americans value the right to bear arms more than human lives. In one scene, Childish Gambino guns down a gospel choir. Many people saw similarities to the 2015 murder of nine African Americans by a white supremacist in a Charleston, South Carolina, church.

Childish Gambino performed "This Is America," wearing a similar outfit yet again to what he wore in the music video, at the 2018 iHeartRadio Music Festival.

protest song, others as a genius piece of art, and still others as offensive nonsense.

The video contains haunting, violent imagery that referenced complex issues, such as the historical oppression of African Americans, guns, police brutality, and technology. The scenes shift jarringly between dancing and violence that include Childish Gambino calmly shooting a faceless victim and gunning down a gospel choir. Throughout the video, cars burn, crowds surge, and horses and police officers run past while the dancers continue dancing and bystanders record the chaos on their cell phones. With no clear answers, viewers were left with countless theories and interpretations.

While some viewers praised the video as a masterpiece, other commentators from both sides of the political spectrum criticized it. Writing in *Spin*, Israel Daramola called the music video "heavy-handed," adding, "It is pandering to the current cultural climate's need for art, particularly black art, to be serious, woke, and important without actually having anything to say."[10] According to Daramola, Childish Gambino was depicting violence against African Americans as entertainment. Meanwhile, some conservative critics saw it as anti-gun propaganda.

JIM CROW POSE

At the beginning of the "This Is America" music video, Childish Gambino smiles and strikes an exaggerated pose with gun in hand. Viewers pointed out that he seemed to be mirroring the pose of a Jim Crow caricature of African Americans popular in the 1800s. In the 1830s, a white traveling actor dressed up in blackface to portray a minstrel character called Jim Crow, which mocked and stereotyped African Americans. The so-called Jim Crow laws enforced segregation in the southern United States in the late 1800s and early 1900s.

"This Is America" won a 2018 MTV Video Music Award for Video with a Message. The video's choreographer, Sherrie Silver, accepted it on behalf of Childish Gambino.

For his part, Glover was slow to offer details and initially gave a tongue-in-cheek explanation: "I just wanted to make, you know, a good song. Something people could play on the Fourth of July."[11] He told late-night television host Jimmy Kimmel a few days later that he had been avoiding the online discussions and analysis of the song.

SUCCESS AND SORROW

Childish Gambino had his first Number 1 single with "This is America." The video captured more than 100 million views in just nine days.[12] Later in the summer, he released two more tracks, "Summertime Magic" and "Feels Like Summer" as part of the *Summer Pack* EP. The animated music video for "Feels Like Summer" referenced the impact of climate change and featured dozens of African American figures as cartoons, from Michelle Obama to Kanye West. Pointing to the stir Glover was causing, *USA Today* called him "the biggest star in the universe right now."[13]

Although Glover saw many accomplishments throughout the year, he dealt with personal tragedy too. In December, Childish Gambino's four-month This Is America tour wrapped up with sold-out, back-to-back shows in Los Angeles. He announced to the crowd that his father had died a few weeks earlier. "I wanted to play him some of the new songs, but he didn't want to hear them, because he was like, 'I know they'll be great.' I'm not saying that to talk about music. I say that to talk about trust."[14] Glover also referenced losing others who were important to him during the year before previewing a track from what was to be Childish Gambino's final album.

DEFYING EXPECTATIONS

At the 2019 Grammys, Childish Gambino's "This Is America" won in all four categories for which it was nominated: Record of the Year, Song of the Year, Best Rap/Sung Performance, and Best Music Video. It was the first rap song to ever win Record of the Year or Song of the Year. Additionally, the track "Feels Like Summer" was nominated for Best R&B Song. Childish Gambino was noticeably absent from the January awards show.

Fans were eagerly awaiting the artist's newest creation. The previous year, Glover and Barbados-born pop star Rihanna reportedly had a secret project in the works together, which had been code named "Dionysus," the name of a Greek god. According to producer Carmen Cuba, the secrecy was necessary. "Everything about this project and Donald, in general in terms of his intentions for his life and his career, is to protect his freedom;

Though Glover claimed that his days as Childish Gambino were almost over, he made many red carpet and event appearances throughout 2018 and 2019.

SONG OF THE YEAR

Although Childish Gambino was nowhere to be found at the 2019 Grammy awards, he made history with his win of Song of the Year, along with cowriters Ludwig Göransson and Jeffery Lamar Williams. They beat contenders who wrote songs for Kendrick Lamar and SZA ("All the Stars"); Ella Mai ("Boo'd Up"); Drake ("God's Plan"); Shawn Mendes ("In My Blood"); Brandi Carlile ("The Joke"); Zedd, Maren Morris, and Grey ("The Middle"); and Lady Gaga and Bradley Cooper ("Shallow").

freedom of expression and freedom of process," she said.[1] At a performance in late 2018, Childish Gambino fueled speculation when he showed what appeared to be a trailer for a movie called *Guava Island*.

Finally, in April 2019, Childish Gambino premiered the project at the popular Coachella Valley Music and Arts Festival in Indio, California, where he was one of the headlining acts. The hour-long film *Guava Island* featured him starring alongside Rihanna. Directed by Murai and written by Stephen Glover, the film was shot on location in Cuba, which stood in for the fictional tropical island of Guava. *Guava Island* contained direct connections to "This Is America" and included characters speaking in lyrics from the song. Many viewers interpreted the film to be a commentary on America, freedom, and oppression.

The film generally earned good reviews, although some critics viewed it as a self-indulgent ending to Glover's Childish Gambino career. "If he'd done this film without the final leg of his Childish Gambino career . . . it'd be insufferable," wrote Anna Menta in the *Decider*. "But Glover has earned this one, and it feels like an apt goodbye."[2]

MUSIC, MOVIES, AND TECHNOLOGY

Meanwhile, Glover was continuing his work on his various projects, though with some delays. In early 2019, it was announced that the third season of *Atlanta* was behind schedule. The CEO of FX, John Landgraf, explained that Glover had been dealing with a foot injury as well as family issues. "As you might imagine, Donald Glover is sort of the king of all media, and he just has had an incredibly complicated life,"

A DIFFICULT YEAR

At his 2019 Coachella performance as Childish Gambino, Glover referenced the difficult personal losses he had experienced in recent months, including the death of his father in late 2018 and the deaths of fellow rappers and friends Mac Miller and Nipsey Hussle. "What I'm starting to realize—all we really have is memories at the end of the day. That's all we are," he told the crowd. "While you're here, while we're here, feel something and pass it on."[3]

In July 2019, Glover, *second from right*, appeared at a press conference for *The Lion King* along with other cast members and director Jon Favreau, *right*.

Landgraf said. Acknowledging that fans and critics were eager for the show's return, he added, "You just have to make a decision about quantity over quality at a certain point, and we're just erring on the side of quality."[4]

In April 2019, Childish Gambino released a new track, "Algorythm," through the launch of an augmented reality (AR) app called "PHAROS AR." The app, described as "the world's first cross-platform, multiplayer

AR music experience," allowed users to explore a computer-generated universe and unlock music.[5] The app developers said the app gave fans from all over the world an entirely new way to interact with Childish Gambino's music.

Then, in July, Glover starred as Simba in the live-action film *The Lion King*, along with Beyoncé as Nala, Seth Rogan as Pumbaa, Billy Eichner as Timon, Chiwetel Ejiofor as

Glover plays Simba, *right*, in the 2019 live-action film *The Lion King*. The movie is based on an earlier animated Disney movie from 1994.

Scar, and James Earl Jones as Mufasa. Glover admitted the process of recording alongside superstar Beyoncé was a little intimidating, but he said it was a special experience.

AN ARTIST FOR THE AGES

The release of new music and associated technology prompted some to question Childish Gambino's supposed retirement. Some fans wondered if he would be retiring entirely from music or solely from his Childish Gambino alter ego.

From an early age, Glover has defied expectations and stereotypes as he carved out an identity for himself. Rather than follow a prescribed track or single passion, Glover tells stories and expresses himself through acting, comedy, music, writing, and directing. This has translated to an incredibly successful career spanning multiple industries. By being true to himself, he has secured his place as a unique performer and creator with something worth saying.

Glover has used Childish Gambino as a way of expressing his insecurities, his frustrations, and his search for meaning. He evolved as an artist and

ADIDAS DEAL

In April 2019, Glover launched a line of Adidas shoes called "Donald Glover Presents." The line included variations of three classic Adidas styles with purposeful imperfections, such as uneven stitching or frayed edges. "Value isn't quantified by what you wear, rather the experiences from them," Glover said. "The [Adidas] partnership for me is about being able to exemplify what doing your own thing truly looks and feels like."[6] As part of the campaign, Glover starred in several minute-long films that also featured actress Mo'Nique and professional skateboarder Na-Kel Smith.

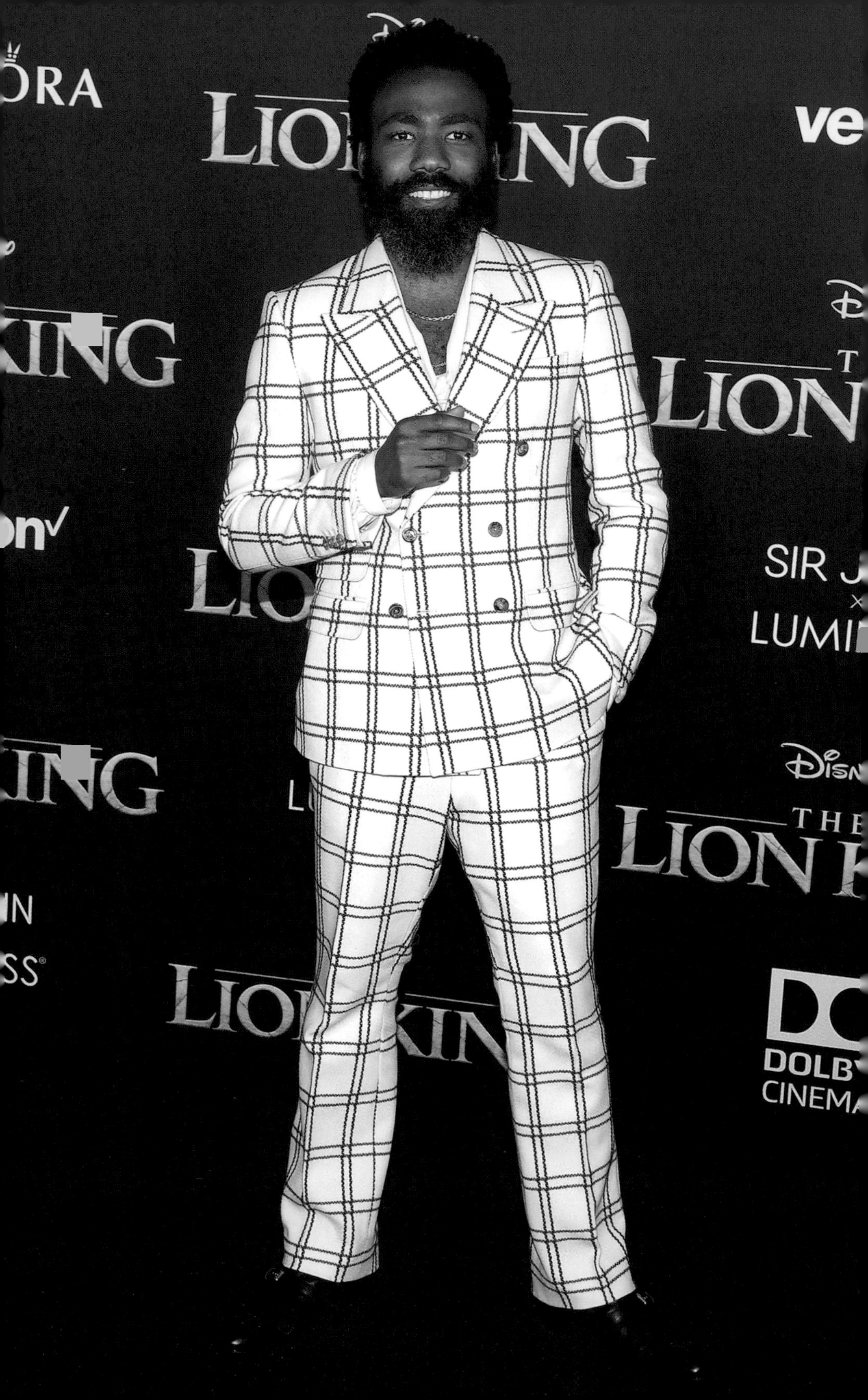
LION
DOLBY
CINEMA

Glover sang several songs as Simba on *The Lion King*'s soundtrack, including "Hakuna Matata" and "Can You Feel the Love Tonight."

learned to follow his own path as he incorporated various musical styles, high-tech visuals, new technology, and immersive fan experiences to create something the industry had not seen before.

Glover didn't have immediate success and will likely never receive universal acclaim, but his work has made the world take notice. He has won both ardent fans and outspoken critics as he sparks discussion around complex issues and offers new perspectives on race in America. Whatever the future holds, there is no doubt that he will continue creating. No one knows exactly what to expect next, and that is just how Glover wants it.

EMBRACING ENDINGS

Glover has embraced endings throughout his career, consistently deciding to move forward with new projects and leave others behind. While talking about creating his Childish Gambino musical identity in 2017, Glover said that people have a difficult time seeing an artist as being talented at more than one thing. "Music is important to me, no question," he said. "Music is one of the loves of my life. But there isn't one thing I'd do forever. I don't believe in things forever."[7]

1983

On September 25, Donald Glover is born at Edwards Air Force Base, California.

2006

Glover gets a job as staff writer for Tina Fey's *30 Rock*.

Glover graduates from the Tisch School of the Arts at New York University (NYU), where he was part of comedy group Derrick Comedy.

2008

In June, Glover releases his first rap mixtape, *Sick Boi*, as his rap alter ego, Childish Gambino.

2009

Glover leaves *30 Rock* to pursue stand-up comedy. He joins the cast of the television show *Community* soon after.

2011

Childish Gambino signs with Glassnote Records.

In November, he releases his debut album, *Camp*.

2013

Childish Gambino releases his second album, *Because the Internet*.

2014

Childish Gambino receives his first Grammy nominations—Best Rap Album (*Because the Internet*) and Best Rap Performance for the song "3005."

2015

Glover has supporting roles in a variety of feature films, including *The Martian*.

2016

Glover's television series *Atlanta* premieres on FX to critical acclaim; Glover's son Legend is born.

2017

Glover wins two Emmy awards for the first season of *Atlanta*, becoming the first African American to win for Outstanding Directing for a Comedy Series.

In December, Childish Gambino releases his third album, *"Awaken, My Love!"*, and he says his fourth album will be his last.

2018

In January, Glover and his partner announce the birth of their second son, and Childish Gambino wins his first Grammy award ("Redbone," Best Traditional R&B Performance).

In May, Glover premieres his song and music video for "This Is America," which he performs live on *Saturday Night Live* while also guest hosting the show.

2019

In February, Childish Gambino wins four Grammys for "This Is America": Record of the Year, Song of the Year, Best Rap/Sung Performance, and Best Music Video.

FULL NAME
Donald Glover

DATE OF BIRTH
September 25, 1983

PLACE OF BIRTH
Edwards Air Force Base, California

PARENTS
Donald Glover Sr. and Beverly Glover

CHILDREN
Two sons, born 2016 (Legend) and 2018 (name not publicly revealed as of 2019)

EDUCATION
High school graduate from DeKalb School of the Arts in Georgia. Graduated from Tisch School of the Arts at New York University in 2006.

CAREER HIGHLIGHTS
Glover won Emmy Awards for Outstanding Lead Actor in a Comedy Series (2017) and Outstanding Directing for a Comedy Series (2017) for his work on *Atlanta*. He won Grammy Awards for Record of the Year and Song of the Year in 2019 for "This Is America." He has been an actor in films and television shows including *Community*, *The Martian*, *Spider-Man: Homecoming*, *Solo: A Star Wars Story*, and *The Lion King*.

ALBUMS

Sick Boi (2008), *Poindexter* (2009), *I Am Just a Rapper* (2010),
I Am Just a Rapper 2 (2010), *Culdesac* (2010), *EP* (2011), *Camp* (2011), *Royalty* (2012), *Because the Internet* (2013), *STN MTN / Kauai* (2014), *"Awaken, My Love!"* (2016), *Summer Pack* (2018)

CONTRIBUTION TO HIP-HOP

Childish Gambino challenges rap stereotypes in his appearance, sound, and subject matter. He creates immersive fan experiences using technology, and his music and videos have sparked national conversations around race in America.

CONFLICTS

Childish Gambino has faced various controversies over depictions of violence, such as in the "This Is America" music video. He has also been criticized for objectifying women in song lyrics.

QUOTE

"The thing I imagine myself being in the future doesn't exist yet. . . . It's something different and more, something involving fairness and restoring a sense of honor."

—*Childish Gambino, 2018*

GLOSSARY

A CAPPELLA
Without instruments.

AFFIRMATIVE ACTION
Practices and policies that attempt to improve opportunities for individuals who are part of minority groups.

AUGMENTED REALITY (AR)
An experience that combines computer-generated imagery with the user's real-world environment.

BLACKFACE
Makeup applied to a performer to imitate a stereotype of a black person.

CAMEO
A small but noticeable appearance of a celebrity in a film, play, song, or other art form.

CARICATURE
An imitation of someone by grotesquely exaggerating his or her characteristics.

FREESTYLING
Rapping lyrics that are made up by the performer on the spot.

IMPROVISATIONAL
Created without preparation.

INDIE
Not belonging to a major record company.

MINSTREL

A traveling performer. Minstrel shows in the United States in the 1800s often used crude racial stereotypes for humor.

MISOGYNY

Hatred of or contempt for women.

MIXTAPE

A compilation of unreleased tracks, freestyle rap music, and DJ mixes of songs.

POLYGLOT

A person who knows several languages.

SEGREGATION

The practice of separating groups of people based on race, gender, ethnicity, or other factors.

SUPREMACIST

Someone who believes people of a particular race, religion, or other category are better than other people.

TOKENIZED

Being included because of one's membership in a minority group to give the appearance of equality.

VIRTUAL REALITY (VR)

Computer-generated simulation of a three-dimensional environment.

SELECTED BIBLIOGRAPHY

Friend, Tad. "Donald Glover Can't Save You," *The New Yorker*, 6 Apr. 2019. newyorker.com. Accessed 5 Apr. 2019.

Jensen, Bill. "Donald Glover is More Talented Than You," *The Village Voice*, 13 Apr. 2011, villagevoice.com. Accessed 6 Apr. 2019.

Lee, Chris. "Donald Glover, Renaissance Man of Comedy and Rap," *Los Angeles Times*, 19 July 2010, latimes.com. Accessed 19 Apr. 2019.

Samuels, Allison. "Inside the Weird, Industry-Shaking World of Donald Glover," *Wired*, 19 Jan. 2017, wired.com. Accessed 5 Apr. 2019.

FURTHER READINGS

Bailey, Diane. *Chance the Rapper: Independent Innovator*. Abdo, 2018.

Lusted, Marcia Amidon. *Hip-Hop Music*. Abdo, 2018.

ONLINE RESOURCES

 Booklinks

NONFICTION NETWORK

FREE! ONLINE NONFICTION RESOURCES

To learn more about Childish Gambino, please visit abdobooklinks.com or scan this QR code. These links are routinely monitored and updated to provide the most current information available.

MORE INFORMATION

For more information on this subject, contact or visit the following organizations:

RCA RECORDS
25 Madison Avenue
New York, NY 10010
rcarecords.com

RCA Records is a record label owned by Sony Music Entertainment. Its artists include A$AP Rocky, Britney Spears, Childish Gambino, and Miley Cyrus.

RECORDING ACADEMY
3030 Olympic Boulevard
Santa Monica, California 90404
grammy.com

The Recording Academy is an organization for musicians, songwriters, producers, and others who work in the music industry. It hosts and decides the winners of the Grammy Awards and also runs MusiCares, which provides funding and other support to music artists in need.

STONE MOUNTAIN PARK
Stone Mountain Park
PO Box 778
Stone Mountain Park, GA 30086
stonemountainpark.com

Stone Mountain Park is a state park near Atlanta, Georgia. The Confederate memorial relief on the side of the mountain has inspired controversy. Visitors can take a cable car to the top of the mountain.

SOURCE NOTES

CHAPTER 1. "THIS IS AMERICA"

1. "Childish Gambino – 'This Is America' SNL Performance." *Dailymotion*, n.d., dailymotion.com. Accessed 26 Aug. 2019.
2. "Childish Gambino – 'This Is America' SNL Performance."
3. "Childish Gambino – 'This Is America' SNL Performance."
4. Joy Press. "*Atlanta* Is the Best Show on TV and Hiro Murai Is Its Visual Mastermind." *Vanity Fair*, 10 Aug. 2018, vanityfair.com. Accessed 26 Aug. 2019.
5. Rachel DeSantis. "A Look Back at All the Stars Who Have Doubled as 'Saturday Night Live' Hosts and Musical Guests." *New York Daily News*, 6 May 2018, nydailynews.com. Accessed 6 Apr. 2019.
6. Jessica Klein. "Childish Gambino's 'This Is America' Clocks 55 Million Views in Just Four Days." *Tubefilter*, 9 May 2018, tubefilter.com. Accessed 26 Aug. 2019.
7. Keith Caulfield. "Childish Gambino's Album Sales Rise 419% in Wake of 'This Is America' Release and 'SNL' Performance." *Billboard*, 14 May 2018, billboard.com. Accessed 6 Apr. 2019.
8. Luvvie Ajayi. "This Is America: Donald Glover's Video Is a Gripping Read." *Awesomely Luvvie*, 6 May 2018, awesomelyluvvie.com. Accessed 6 Apr. 2019.
9. @janellemonae. "Donald . Glover ." *Twitter*, 6 May 2018, 12:19 p.m., twitter.com. Accessed 26 Aug. 2019.
10. Bijan Stephen. "Donald Glover, the Man Everyone in Hollywood Wishes They Were." *Esquire*, 15 Aug. 2018, esquire.com. Accessed 26 Aug. 2019.
11. "Childish Gambino – 'This Is America' SNL Performance."

CHAPTER 2. LOOKING TO SAVE THE WORLD

1. Billy Nilles. "Everything We Still Don't Know about Donald Glover's Remarkably Private Life." *E! News*, 1 Jan. 2019, eonline.com. Accessed 26 Apr. 2019.
2. Bijan Stephen. "Donald Glover Has Always Been Ten Steps Ahead." *Esquire*, 7 Feb. 2018, esquire.com. Accessed 5 Apr. 2019.
3. Stephen, "Donald Glover Has Always Been Ten Steps Ahead."
4. Spencer Kornhaber. "Wiseguy." *Spin*, May 2011, www.spin.com. Accessed 26 Aug. 2019.
5. Dan Wilcox. "Donald Glover." *KCRW*, 11 May 2011, kcrw.com. Accessed 26 Aug. 2019.
6. Wilcox, "Donald Glover."
7. Josh Eells. "Donald Glover: The Triple Threat." *Rolling Stone*, 7 Sept. 2011, rollingstone.com. Accessed 26 Aug. 2019.
8. Laura Fitzpatrick. "Brief History of YouTube." *Time*, 31 May 2010, content.time.com. Accessed 26 Aug. 2019.

CHAPTER 3. BIG BREAKS

1. Tad Friend. "Donald Glover Can't Save You." *New Yorker*, 6 Apr. 2019, newyorker.com. Accessed 5 Apr. 2019.
2. Jacob Moore. "Know the Ledge." *Complex*, Feb./Mar. 2014, complex.com. Accessed 26 Aug. 2019.
3. Daniel Holloway. "Note to SNL: Black People Are Funny, Too." *HuffPost*, 25 Feb. 2008, huffpost.com. Accessed 26 Aug. 2019.
4. "Childish Gambino: My Hoodie." *AZ Lyrics*, n.d., azlyrics.com. Accessed 26 Aug. 2019.
5. Chris Lee. "Donald Glover, Renaissance Man of Comedy and Rap." *Los Angeles Times*, 19 July 2010, latimes.com. Accessed 26 Aug. 2019.
6. Nev Pierce. "'Atlanta' Creator/Star Donald Glover on 'Cresting' in His Career." *Deadline*, 7 June 2017, deadline.com. Accessed 1 May 2019.
7. Megan Angelo. "His Day Job Subsidizes All That Other Stuff." *New York Times*, 10 Mar. 2010, nytimes.com. Accessed 26 Aug. 2019.
8. Amos Barshad. "Overachiever: Donald Glover." *New York Magazine*, 25 Nov. 2009, nymag.com. Accessed 6 Apr. 2019.
9. Angelo, "His Day Job Subsidizes All That Other Stuff."

10. Bijan Stephen. "Donald Glover Has Always Been Ten Steps Ahead." *Esquire*, 7 Feb. 2018, esquire.com. Accessed 5 Apr. 2019.

11. Angelo, "His Day Job Subsidizes All That Other Stuff."

12. Mark Olsen. "Comedy Group's Charming Effort." *Los Angeles Times*, 12 Mar. 2010, latimes.com. Accessed 1 Apr. 2019.

CHAPTER 4. SUPERHEROES AND MIXTAPES

1. Cyriaque Lamar. "Smilin' Stan Lee Weighs in on Donald Glover for Spider-Man." *Io9*, 9 June 2010, io9.gizmodo.com. Accessed 17 Apr. 2019.

2. Rick Marshall. "Donald Glover Says He Was 'Floored' by 'Spider-Man' Fan Campaign." *MTV News*, 23 June 2010, mtv.com. Accessed 26 Aug. 2019.

3. Chris Lee. "Donald Glover, Renaissance Man of Comedy and Rap." *Los Angeles Times*, 19 July 2010, latimes.com. Accessed 26 Aug. 2019.

4. Lee, "Donald Glover, Renaissance Man of Comedy and Rap."

5. Bill Jensen. "Donald Glover Is More Talented Than You," *Village Voice*, 13 Apr. 2011, villagevoice.com. Accessed 6 Apr. 2019.

6. Abe Schwartz. "A Review of Donald Glover's Debut Rap Album, 'Culdesac.'" *HuffPost*, 7 Sept. 2011, huffpost.com. Accessed 26 Aug. 2019.

7. Nicole James. "We HAVE to Say Something about Donald Glover/Childish Gambino's 'Freaks and Geeks.'" *MTV News*, 28 Feb. 2011, mtv.com. Accessed 28 Apr. 2019.

8. Lee, "Donald Glover, Renaissance Man of Comedy and Rap."

9. Justin Ward. "Bonnaroo 2011 Lineup." *LIVE Music Blog*, 2 May 2019, livemusicblog.com. Accessed 26 Aug. 2019.

10. Megan Vick. "Childish Gambino Signs with Glassnote Records." *Billboard*, 6 Sept. 2011, billboard.com. Accessed 26 Aug. 2019.

CHAPTER 5. RISING STAR

1. Ian Cohen. "Childish Gambino: *Camp* Album Review." *Pitchfork*, 2 Dec. 2011, pitchfork.com. Accessed 23 Apr. 2019.

2. Michael P. Jeffries. "Drake, Childish Gambino, and the Specter of Black Authenticity," *Atlantic*, 22 Nov. 2011, theatlantic.com. Accessed 19 Apr. 2019.

3. Claire Suddath. "Music Monday: Childish Gambino's *Camp*." *Time*, 14 Nov. 2011, entertainment.time.com. Accessed 26 Aug. 2019.

4. "Childish Gambino: Hold You Down." *Bing*, n.d., bing.com. Accessed 26 Aug. 2019.

5. Caroline Pate. "Here's Why People Think Donald Glover Hates Women." *Bustle*, 16 Oct. 2013, bustle.com. Accessed 19 Apr. 2019.

6. Jeff Niesel. "Concert Review: Childish Gambino at House of Blues." *Scene and Heard*, 18 June 2019, clevescene.com. Accessed 20 Apr. 2019.

7. Dan Wilcox. "Donald Glover." *KCRW*, 11 May 2011, kcrw.com. Accessed 26 Aug. 2019.

8. Corban Goble. "Mixtape of the Week: Childish Gambino 'Royalty.'" *Stereogum*, 11 July 2012, stereogum.com. Accessed 17 Apr. 2019.

9. Chaz Kangas. "Childish Gambino – 'The Younger I Get.'" *Popular Opinions with Chaz Kangas*, 11 Nov. 2011, popularopinions.wordpress.com. Accessed 26 Apr. 2019.

10. Zack Sharf. "Donald Glover's 'Insult of White Women' on 'Girls' Was Improvised." *IndieWire*, 26 Feb. 2018, indiewire.com. Accessed 20 Apr. 2019.

11. Alex Young. "Donald Glover Signs Deal with FX for New Music-Themed Comedy Atlanta." *Consequence of Sound*, 6 Aug. 2013, consequenceofsound.net. Accessed 22 Apr. 2019.

12. Ben Kaye. "Donald Glover Recalls Chevy Chase's Racism on Set of *Community*." *Consequence of Sound*, 26 Feb. 2018, consequenceofsound.net. Accessed 28 Apr. 2019.

13. "Childish Gambino: Figure It Out." *Genius*, n.d., genius.com. Accessed 26 Aug. 2019.

14. Killian Fox. "Childish Gambino: *Because the Internet* Review." *Guardian*, 7 Dec. 2013, theguardian.com. Accessed 20 Apr. 2019.

15. Zach Dionne. "We Went There: Childish Gambino's Deep Web Tour." *Grantland*, 31 Mar. 2014, grantland.com. Accessed 20 Apr. 2019.

SOURCE NOTES

16. Brian Cantor. "Childish Gambino's 'Because the Internet' Earns Gold Certification in US." *Headline Planet*, n.d., headlineplanet.com. Accessed 26 Aug. 2019.

17. Chris Mench. "But I'm Not a Rapper: Everything You Need to Know about Childish Gambino's First Three Mixtapes." *Complex*, 26 Aug. 2015, complex.com. Accessed 30 Apr. 2019.

18. Craig Jenkins. "Childish Gambino: *Because the Internet.*" *Pitchfork*, 12 Dec. 2013, pitchfork.com. Accessed 23 Apr. 2019.

CHAPTER 6. ON TO THE NEXT

1. Chad Roberts. "Interview: Donald Glover Talks Rap Career & Spider-Man Twitter Campaign." *Complex*, 4 Aug. 2010, complex.com. Accessed 26 Aug. 2019.

2. Terri Schwartz. "Donald Glover Explains Why He Didn't Return to *Community.*" *IGN*, 9 Aug. 2016, ign.com. Accessed 26 Apr. 2019.

3. Danielle Harling. "Childish Gambino Explains Why He Called Out Drake, Kendrick Lamar." *Hip Hop DX*, 11 Sept. 2014, hiphopdx.com. Accessed 26 Aug. 2019.

4. Ikenna Anyoku. "Donald Glover Speaks Out on Police Brutality, Twitter Activism, Being White." *Daily Dot*, 15 Aug. 2014, dailydot.com. Accessed 19 Apr. 2019.

5. Anyoku, "Donald Glover Speaks Out."

6. Harling, "Childish Gambino Explains."

7. Patrick Ryan. "Childish Gambino Sees Opportunity in Grammy Nod." *USA Today*, 5 Feb. 2015, usatoday.com. Accessed 30 Apr. 2019.

8. "Childish Gambino: Late Night in Kauai." *Metro Lyrics*, n.d., metrolyrics.com. Accessed 26 Aug. 2019.

9. Michael Madden. "Childish Gambino – *STN MTN / Kauai.*" *Consequence of Sound*, 16 Oct. 2014, consequenceofsound.net. Accessed 23 Apr. 2019.

10. Harling, "Childish Gambino Explains."

11. H. Drew Blackburn. "A Gray Matter: On Donald Glover and Post-Blackness." *Consequence of Sound*, 3 Jan. 2014, consequenceofsound.net. Accessed 23 Apr. 2019.

12. Ryan, "Childish Gambino Sees Opportunity."

13. "Can Someone Explain 'Roscoe's Wetsuit'?" *Reddit: Donaldglover*, 5 Sept. 2013, reddit.com. Accessed 27 Apr. 2019.

14. Cynthia Littleton. "Donald Glover's 'Atlanta' Gets Series Order From FX." *Variety*, 15 Oct. 2015, variety.com. Accessed 20 Apr. 2019.

CHAPTER 7. WELCOME TO ATLANTA

1. Lanre Bakare. "Atlanta: Donald Glover's Show Is the Smartest—and Funniest—on TV." *Guardian*, 19 Oct. 2016, theguardian.com. Accessed 1 May 2019.

2. Matthew Shaer. "Why *Atlanta* Creator Donald Glover Is One of the Most Creative People in Business in 2017." *Fast Company*, 17 May 2017, fastcompany.com. Accessed 6 Apr. 2019.

3. Billy Nilles. "Inside Donald Glover's Effortless Rise to Hollywood Royalty." *E! News*, 10 Sept. 2018, eonline.com. Accessed 21 Apr. 2019.

4. Nev Pierce. "'Atlanta' Creator/Star Donald Glover on 'Cresting' in His Career." *Deadline*, 7 June 2017, deadline.com. Accessed 1 May 2019.

5. Allison Samuels. "Inside the Weird, Industry-Shaking World of Donald Glover." *Wired*, 19 Jan. 2017, wired.com. Accessed 5 Apr. 2019.

6. Samuels, "Inside the Weird, Industry-Shaking World of Donald Glover."

7. Amaya Mendizabal. "Childish Gambino's '*Awaken, My Love!*' Debuts at No. 1 on R&B Albums Chart." *Billboard*, 14 Dec. 2016, billboard.com. Accessed 26 Aug. 2019.

8. Trent Clark. "Jordan Peele Explains Why Childish Gambino's 'Redbone' Was Perfect for 'Get Out.'" *Hip Hop DX*, 23 Feb. 2017, hiphopdx.com. Accessed 26 Aug. 2019.

9. "Donald Glover AKA Childish Gambino—2018 Grammys Full Backstage Interview." *YouTube*, uploaded by Variety, 29 Jan. 2018, youtube.com. Accessed 26 Aug. 2019.

10. Shaer, "Why *Atlanta* Creator Donald Glover Is One of the Most Creative People in Business in 2017."

11. Khal. "Donald Glover's Pop Culture Domination Is Unprecedented." *Complex*, 12 May 2017, complex.com. Accessed 26 Aug. 2019.

12. Billy Nilles. "Everything We Still Don't Know about Donald Glover's Remarkably Private Life." *E! News*, 1 Jan. 2019, eonline.com. Accessed 26 Apr. 2019.

13. Taryn Finley. "Donald Glover Reveals Why He's Retiring Childish Gambino." *HuffPost*, 6 June 2017, huffpost.com. Accessed 1 May 2019.

14. Tina Fey. "Donald Glover." *Time*, 2017, time.com. Accessed 19 Apr. 2019.

CHAPTER 8. THE YEAR OF DONALD

1. Tad Friend. "Donald Glover Can't Save You." *New Yorker*, 6 Apr. 2019, newyorker.com. Accessed 26 Aug. 2019.

2. Greg Evans. "'Atlanta' Trailer: New Season, New Name, New Threats." *Deadline*, 13 Feb. 2018, deadline.com. Accessed 26 Aug. 2019.

3. Patrick Hipes. "FX's 'Atlanta Robbin' Season' Bow Earns Strong Ratings." *Deadline*, 7 Mar. 2018, deadline.com. Accessed 26 Aug. 2019.

4. Megh Wright. "'Atlanta,' 'Horace and Pete,' 'Better Things,' and 'Veep' Win Peabody Awards." *Vulture*, 20 Apr. 2017, vulture.com. Accessed 26 Aug. 2019.

5. Kyle Buchanan. "*Solo* Needed Way More of Donald Glover's Lando." *Vulture*, 30 May 2018, vulture.com. Accessed 23 Apr. 2019.

6. Patrick Cavanaugh. "Donald Glover Jokes That Scoring Lando Part in 'Solo' Makes Him Look Like a 'Mary Sue.'" *Comicbook*, 8 Feb. 2018, comicbook.com. Accessed 26 Aug. 2019.

7. Bijan Stephen. "Donald Glover Has Always Been Ten Steps Ahead." *Esquire*, 7 Feb. 2018, esquire.com. Accessed 5 Apr. 2019.

8. Lawrence Burney. "Donald Glover Likes to Imagine if 'Atlanta' Was Just Made for Black People." *Vice*, 26 Feb. 2018, vice.com. Accessed 26 Aug. 2019.

9. Zack Sharf. "Donald Glover's Answer to Why He Made 'This Is America' Is On Point." *IndieWire*, 9 May 2018, indiewire.com. Accessed 28 Apr. 2019.

10. Israel Daramola. "The Cynicism of Childish Gambino's 'This Is America.'" *Spin*, 8 May 2018, spin.com. Accessed 2 May 2019.

11. Brian Bell. "Donald Glover Opens Up about His 'This Is America' Music Video, Portraying Lando Calrissian." *Paste*, 11 May 2018, pastemagazine.com. Accessed 26 Aug. 2019.

12. Hayley Miller. "Childish Gambino's 'Feels Like Summer' Video Imagines Kanye West, Rihanna as Cartoons." *HuffPost*, 2 Sept. 2018, huffpost.com. Accessed 2 May 2019.

13. Brian Alexander. "How Donald Glover's Lando Calrissian Stole 'Solo: A Star Wars Story.'" *USA Today*, 21 May 2018, usatoday.com. Accessed 21 Apr. 2019.

14. Michael Saponara. "Donald Glover Finishes Tour by Honoring Late Father, Playing Unreleased Music." *Billboard*, 18 Dec. 2018, billboard.com. Accessed 2 May 2018.

CHAPTER 9. DEFYING EXPECTATIONS

1. Kelly Wynne. "What Is 'Guava Island'? Everything We Know about Donald Glover's Secret Amazon Prime Project, How to Watch and Rihanna's Involvement." *Newsweek*, 11 Apr. 2019, newsweek.com. Accessed 1 May 2019.

2. Anna Menta. "Stream It or Skip It: 'Guava Island' on Prime Video." *Decider*, 13 Apr. 2019, decider.com. Accessed 2 May 2019.

3. Michael Blackmon. "Donald Glover Cried Onstage at Coachella Talking about Mac Miller and Nipsey Hussle." *Buzzfeed News*, 14 Apr. 2019, buzzfeednews.com. Accessed 1 May 2019.

4. "'Atlanta' Season 3 Delayed at FX." *Billboard*, 4 Feb. 2019, billboard.com. Accessed 2 May 2019.

5. Zack Ruskin. "Childish Gambino Premieres New Song 'Algorythm' with AR App Bringing Concert Experience to Mobile Devices." *Billboard*, 24 Apr. 2019, billboard.com. Accessed 2 May 2019.

6. Peter Helman. "Childish Gambino Launches Adidas Line with a Bunch of Short Films." *Stereogum*, 18 Apr. 2019, stereogum.com. Accessed 2 May 2019.

7. Nev Pierce. "'Atlanta' Creator/Star Donald Glover on 'Cresting' in His Career." *Deadline*, 7 June 2017, deadline.com. Accessed 1 May 2019.

Laura K. Murray has written more than 65 nonfiction books about subjects ranging from music and pop culture to history and science. She lives in Minnesota.